Praise for *The Compassionate Hunter's Guidebook*

The Compassionate Hunter's Guidebook helps the reader embrace the most basic truth of our existence—that life cannot exist without death. Buying meat on a Styrofoam tray insulates us from that reality. Avoiding meat is potentially worse, as ecosystems are degraded and wildlife habitat is lost to the plow. Olson encourages readers to take life into their own hands by *hunting from the heart*. He provides A-to-Z instructions to embrace reality and discover the most balanced way to sustain ourselves and the planet.

> — Thomas J. Elpel, author, *Participating in Nature* and producer, *The Art of Nothing* Wilderness Survival Video Series

Arguably the food that most closely approximates our nutritional needs, wild game assumes a sacred and satiating beauty in *The Compassionate Hunter*. If you've ever wondered how people could reverence hunting, Miles Olson explains the whole relationship the way it ought to be. That makes all the difference.

> — Joel Salatin, farmer and author

This is not your typical hunting manual. Olson's practical advice on how to hunt and utilize animals fully—where else will you find a recipe for a dessert made from deerskin?—are framed by the vital recognition that every being is bound up in the same sacred web of life and death. Earthy and heartfelt, this book reminds us that hunting provides sustenance for both body and soul, and that mindful eating requires both respect and gratitude.

> —Tovar Cerulli, author, *The Mindful Carnivore: A Vegetarian's Hunt for Sustenance*

The
Compassionate
Hunter's
GUIDEBOOK

The Compassionate Hunter's GUIDEBOOK

Hunting from the Heart

Miles Olson

new society
PUBLISHERS

New Society Publishers acknowledges the financial support of the Government of
Canada through the Canada Book Fund (CBF) for our publishing activities.

Inquiries regarding requests to reprint all or part of *The Compassionate Hunter's
Guidebook* should be addressed to New Society Publishers at the address below.

To order directly from the publishers, please call toll-free (North America)
1-800-567-6772, or order online at www.newsociety.com

Any other inquiries can be directed by mail to:
New Society Publishers
P.O. Box 189, Gabriola Island, BC V0R 1X0, Canada
(250) 247-9737

LIBRARY AND ARCHIVES CANADA CATALOGUING IN PUBLICATION

Olson, Miles, author
The compassionate hunter's guidebook : hunting from
the heart / Miles Olson.

Includes bibliographical references and index.
Issued in print and electronic formats.
ISBN 978-0-86571-770-1 (pbk.). — ISBN 978-1-55092-553-1 (ebook)

1. Hunting. 2. Hunting—Moral and ethical aspects. 3. Game
and game-birds, Dressing of. 4. Cooking (Game). I. Title.
II. Title: Hunter's guidebook.

SK36.9.O47 2014   799.2   C2014-900434-6
                                       C2014-900435-4

New Society Publishers' mission is to publish books that contribute in fundamental
ways to building an ecologically sustainable and just society, and to do so with the
least possible impact on the environment, in a manner that models this vision. We
are committed to doing this not just through education, but through action. The
interior pages of our bound books are printed on Forest Stewardship Council®-
registered acid-free paper that is 100% post-consumer recycled (100% old growth
forest-free), processed chlorine-free, and printed with vegetable-based, low-VOC
inks, with covers produced using FSC®-registered stock. New Society also works to
reduce its carbon footprint, and purchases carbon offsets based on an annual audit
to ensure a carbon neutral footprint. For further information, or to browse our
full list of books and purchase securely, visit our website at: www.newsociety.com

new society
PUBLISHERS

MIX
Paper from
responsible sources
FSC® C016245

Mississippi Mills
Public Library

Contents

1

The Compassionate Hunter

It's a cold November morning. A thin layer of snow covers the forest floor, reflecting the silver light of the moon. I have been sitting silently in my hunting spot for maybe 15 minutes, trying to be as still as possible. The forest, however, feels anything but still. There might not be a more active, intense time all year in these woods than this window of time during the annual mating season, or "rut." Bucks are roaming the woods chasing the scent of fertile does with little regard for anything other than sex and establishing dominance. Does, likewise, are less cautious as they start to ovulate and their bodies fill with excitement for a partner. Their changing scent will bring in potential lovers. For a time this annual dance of courtship and intimacy eclipses all else. For a while the deer are possessed by an insatiable urge.

As I sit shiftlessly in the woods, the feeling is palpable. The forest is quiet, but there is an overwhelming sense of activity, electricity and excitement silently buzzing through it. Maybe I'm imagining it because of all the activity I've seen over the past couple days in the forest; either way I can feel it. My eyes are wide open, watching. My ears soak in every noise with anticipation. On mornings like this, it is somehow very easy to sit silently in the woods and stay energized. Even if I don't see any deer, I'll still have harvested a deep feeling of groundedness. After sitting like this for some time, I think I hear something in the distance. A faint crunching of crusty snow.

It's barely audible, far off in the distance, but steadily approaches. I straighten my back, trying to keep still as my anticipation grows. My breath condenses in the freezing air in front of my face, reminding me how cold it is.

The morning light has now fully taken over from the moon, which has dropped out of sight.

The distinctive noise of hooves crunching gets closer as this deer meanders along. It comes into view, through the bushes. It's a buck, with antlers shaped like two pronged forks rising from his skull. He is heading right along the path that leads by me, and will pass about 20 yards from where I sit as it heads toward a nearby clearing. I should get a clear shot. As I sit, watch and prepare myself, I notice how beautiful he is.

As he approaches, seemingly unaware of my presence, I prepare. I flick my safety off and ready myself for a shot, adrenaline pumping through me. As he comes directly in front of me, I lock my aim over his heart. Then he pauses.

He is probably surveying the area for the source of a sound. I must have made a noise. At the end of a deep exhalation, I squeeze the trigger. He makes a sudden bucking movement, digging his hooves into the ground, and bounds into the bush.

For the next thirty minutes I stay put, not wanting to spook the deer and cause him to run farther if he has bedded down nearby and is alive. When enough time has passed (and it feels like an eternity), I get up and walk to the spot where the deer was standing when I shot. There is blood staining the snow, accompanied by some hair, too. I definitely hit him. On this morning the snow is my dear friend, as it holds a trail of blood that may lead me very clearly to my prey.

I only have to follow the patchy, red-stained path for a couple minutes before I come upon him, collapsed amid the protection of a thicket of salmonberry bushes. His body is motionless, tongue sticking out of his mouth, eyes wide open. He appears to be dead. Still, this is a large, strong creature, so I grab a fallen branch and gently touch him with it in tender spots—his mouth, his belly, an eye—testing for a reaction. There isn't any, but I still stand and wait a few minutes before going any closer.

I stare at his body, his body that had been so full of life just a few minutes before. I look into his eyes. Eventually I approach him. I get down on my knees and give him a hug. His body is warm, his muscles loose; there are few chances to be so close to such a beautiful, powerful wild creature.

I say a simple "thank you" and admire him for a while longer in silence, before beginning to dismantle his body. I will spend the next several hours working steadily; first gutting my kill, then carrying it home (or, rather, pulling it along the snow and heaving it up over logs and other obstructions), skinning and butchering it right away, before it has time to freeze solid in the ice cold air. Feeling grateful.

I was initially going to call this book *The Ethical Hunter's Guidebook*. It is meant to be an exploration of and guide to hunting from a conscious, ethical perspective. It is a guide for those that come to the act with pure intentions, motivated by a desire for healthy food that comes directly from the land where they live, rather than an incomprehensibly complex industrial food supply; a practical manual that explores the ethics of killing at the same time. There are, after all, countless ethical reasons to point a caring person toward hunting.

Wild meat is more sustainable, comes from a happier, healthier and more ecologically intact place than even the most elegant organic farming can approach. None of the customary manipulation and abuse that humans employ to make the land say *food* (clearing, plowing, irrigating, weeding, fertilizing, spraying, feeding, etc.) are necessary for this nourishment to exist; it's not a product of human meddling. On the contrary, it comes into being of its own will, in accord with the land. Depending on how and where one hunts, the environmental footprint can be tiny. Hunting doesn't support big agribusiness. It's as local as it gets. And, of course, it can be an incredibly valuable resource for individuals and families that want an affordable source of nutritious, local, ethical, grass-fed meat.

Hunting one's own meat also provides one with the most honest, intimate understanding of its true cost. Once one's own hands are stained with blood, the mind and heart are also touched by the complex, humbling and profound reality of this relationship. It was while thinking about this relationship, the dynamic interaction between predator and prey, hunter and hunted, that I realized my initial title for this book, *The Ethical Hunter's Guidebook*, wasn't going to cut it.

Ethics are by definition products of the rational mind; logical conclusions about the nature of reality from which we build our sense of right and wrong. They are matters of the intellect—matters of the intellect that are incredibly important and valuable, but we're talking about hunting here. Or, to be more exact, we're talking about *killing and eating*. About life and death; subjects that can only really be approached in all their fullness and complexity by going into the *heart*.

To adequately address the depth of the subject, this had to become a guidebook for *compassionate* hunting; for those who hunt for any or all of the above ethical and economic reasons, but who also feel a sense of deep respect and reverence toward their prey, who are interested in approaching hunting (and all of life) as something sacred.

On one hand this book is a practical guide, filled with basic information that will help beginning hunters approach the act with fundamental knowledge and confidence, and offer even experienced hunters some information on how to use their kill more completely. But it's also about much more. It's about consciously coming into contact with death and how that death is transformed into our bodies and into life. It's about acknowledging and embracing aspects of reality that our society has become disconnected from. It's about breaking ourselves open to a sacred experience that is completely grounded in the fabric of our lives; in the food we eat and how we get it.

Compassion and hunting

I can honestly say that the deer I described at the beginning of this chapter, who I quietly spied on that cold November morning, was one of the most beautiful creatures I have ever seen. He was one of the most beautiful creatures I have ever seen, and yet I killed him. This sounds like a terrible mistake, like it never should have happened at all. But there is a place deep inside me that knows it was right, a place that knows it made complete sense. I saw that deer in its aliveness, grace and beauty. I felt admiration and respect for him. And I then extinguished that flame of life. To nourish my own. This is a relationship that feeds, humbles and fascinates me. It's also the paradox of compassion and hunting.

A friend recently told me how ironic it is that some of the most impressive conservation work being done in the US is funded by organizations made up of hunters. How bizarre, she remarked, that the people preserving and protecting habitat for wild creatures are the very ones who make a pastime out of killing them. As a hunter, I didn't find this bizarre or surprising at all; hunters have more directly invested in the preservation of healthy wild ecosystems than most other people. As someone who at one time was not a hunter, and who still remembers the popular conceptions and misconceptions around what that label means, however, I completely understood what she was saying.

Many people have a picture of the *hunter* in their imaginations that looks a bit like this: a macho, male, aggressive, over-stimulated, gun-toting redneck who likes to blow the heads off of innocent wild creatures for kicks. Someone with no respect for nature or life. Now, I have to acknowledge that this image is based on a certain level of truth. The fact is, there is a spectrum of hunters, a spectrum of what hunting can be and can mean. On one end of this spectrum are people who head into the bush to shoot something just for the thrill of it. That's all. They might have a picture taken posing proudly beside the grizzly bear or bull moose they have slain to document their impressive feat. They do not eat any of this animal, they just take its life for fun, as if it was a character in a video game. While this kind of conduct represents just a tiny fraction of hunters, and is illegal in many states, it does still happen. Then you have hunters who actually take the meat from the creatures they kill for eating, and at the very other end of this spectrum you have those who use all of the meat, bones, fat, organs and skin of their prey, when possible. These subsistence hunters aren't hunting for "sport," and the creatures whose lives they take are not part of a "game." They are hunting so they can eat, and taking personal responsibility for all that entails with humility and respect. They have a deep respect for the animals they kill, since their own sustenance depends on those very animals. This book is about those hunters and that kind of hunting.

Hearing stories about disrespectful hunters and declaring that hunting is wrong is about as thoughtful as seeing pornography and deciding that sex is wrong. Both acts can be beautiful, sacred things, but both can also be senseless, oppressive and outright ugly. Which direction they go in has less to do with the simple, mechanical act itself and more to do with how it is approached; the integrity, empathy and respect of those involved. Hunting itself is neither inherently good or bad. It can be a very humane and responsible way of getting food. It also has an inherent potential to crack the heart of the hunter open, to stir up from the depths of their being huge questions about the nature of life and existence. But it can also be as shallow and disconnected from emotional and energetic reality as pornography is. This all depends on perception and empathy; on whether or not the hunter is open to *seeing* their prey as a sentient being worthy of respect, *feeling* the depth of what is really going on when they choose to take its life and fully honoring the sanctity of that life.

Take, for example, the "sport" of catch-and-release fishing. Every fall I sit on the banks of my local river during the salmon run and watch, in a kind of disbelief, this strange phenomenon. If you aren't familiar with catch and release, it is a type of recreational fishing where one catches a fish, then carefully reels it in as it struggles and fights against you, pulling with all of its force against the metal hook that has pierced its mouth or lodged into its body. Depending on the size and species, this struggle can take a good few minutes. Once you have successfully landed the fish, pulling it into your boat or dragging it onto the land, you remove the hook from its face or body and toss it back into the water from which it came, a little bruised, battered and torn.

In the fall as I sit on the riverbank and watch this strange phenomenon—dozens of grown men in hip waders torturing fish for fun—I wonder to myself: *What the hell is going on here?* Fish are not characters in a video game—they are living beings that feel pain. What are these guys doing?

This is where perception and empathy make a difference. Presumably the anglers that play this game with unfortunate fish don't see the fish as having feelings, as being sentient. Or, if they do, they don't see that as mattering. They don't empathize with the fish; they don't at any level feel what the fish feels, cringe at the pain they are subjecting it to for no reason besides entertainment. What is really interesting about this is that most of the men I have watched practising catch-and-release fishing are passionate nature lovers, naturalists and outdoorsmen who truly love getting out and being in the wild. These are men who have a great deal of knowledge and respect for the natural world, men who are generally very kind people yet somehow have a certain inner switch that has been turned off with regards to these fish; the switch that controls empathy.

I am interested in living with that switch flipped on, because one experiences a shallower level of reality otherwise. Those fish *do* feel pain. And, in the context of hunting, when we kill something, we *are* taking the life of a sentient being out of this world, something beautiful and worthy of reverence and respect. If we don't acknowledge and open ourselves to this reality, our experience is just a fraction of the truth. To approach hunting (and all of life) with an open, compassionate heart is the only way one can actually experience its full reality. It is this subtle difference in perception and empathy that distinguishes what I call the *compassionate* hunter. And despite popular perceptions that would suggest otherwise, a great deal of hunters fall into this category.

Compassion, of course, is not something people typically associate with hunting. After all, killing animals and having compassion for them don't really add up, do they? The answer to this question is complicated, but my own journey and experiences have given me plenty of insight into it. Whenever I am confronted by this question, my first thought is that we might be asking the wrong question. A better question may be: *Is there any way of living that* doesn't *require death to sustain it? Is there really an escape from this dilemma, or is it actually hardwired into this reality; an inescapable, integral and (nowadays) hidden part of everyone's sustenance that hunting simply makes obvious?*

Yes, that's a better question.

Hunting is different from other ways we get food because the associated cost, the loss of life, is made unmistakably, unavoidably apparent. Hunting means killing. It means blood and death. There's no escaping it.

Buying a loaf of bread or a brick of tofu, however, don't appear to have anything to do with this harsh reality. But if we go beneath the surface, the idea that these foods are somehow less harsh, less costly to life, quickly reveals itself to be an illusion. Allow me to explain.

There are in fact countless invisible lives that are extinguished as a by-product of modern farming; combine harvesters alone (used to harvest grain crops) are responsible for mincing any rodent, groundhog, snake or other unfortunate creature in their path during harvest. These lives are invisible to us and disappear unnoticed. They are collateral damage. This fact alone pops the bubble of guilt-free eating that many vegetarians might live in.

I want to dig a bit deeper than this, though.

It is an incredible thing that wild animals such as deer are the product of a rich, healthy, wild ecosystem. It is incredible that one can sustainably harvest food from such a place. Indeed, harvesting some animals, in some instances, is very beneficial to their home ecology. The reason I find this so incredible is that most of the food we as a society eat comes from a place that is almost the exact opposite. In order for a field of corn, soy, tomatoes or wheat to exist you need to actually remove a healthy, intact, wild ecosystem. You need to eliminate habitat for many wild animals (and, consequently, the lives of many wild animals, since their population is a function of food supply, aka habitat), not to mention the lives and homes of countless other wild plants, insects and so on, in order to plant your chosen species. There is no land that is simply sitting, empty, waiting to be planted and cultivated by the hands of humans. You have to make it produce, and this process, if we extend our empathy to all of those unwanted plants and animals that need to be removed or killed in order for it to happen, begins to level out any moral superiority the farmer might have thought they had over the hunter.

Within this framework, hunting is actually incredibly graceful. The only moment where the flow of life is disrupted is the very last: the moment of the kill. For every other moment of its life, the hunter's prey lives in a state of completely unhindered wildness and freedom, wandering through distant lands, looking for love in all the wrong places and sometimes the right ones. In farming, on the other hand, the flow of life is disrupted from beginning to end, and in the end there is still a death, even if it's only a carrot that is killed.

My point here is not to make a case that hunting or gathering wild plants are morally superior to other ways of getting food, but that nourishing ourselves involves a loss of life, some kind of death or killing, *any* way we do it. This is one of the great paradoxes of being alive and being human, and one that hunting, because of its explicit connection to this truth, brings us face to face with.

The hunter knows exactly what the cost of their meat is; they saw the whole story unfold with their own eyes. The consumer, on the other hand, can never really know how to measure the true cost of their food, what pain and loss might have been part of its creation. There is a safety in this, a protection from disquieting truths, but it's the safety of ignorance. In this sense hunting is more honest, more raw.

In the coming pages, I hope to fully embrace the two sides of the act of hunting that I have touched upon here. This book is filled with practical, how-to information, but it also has that switch I mentioned earlier, the one that controls empathy, turned on, because otherwise it would only be holding a hollow shell of the truth. Hunting can connect us in a very deep way to the web of life, to a reality that is pure, that is grounded in the timelessness of the earth and the processes of creation that furnish our sustenance. Killing creatures for food has fed and continues to feed me on many levels, and has also challenged and continues to challenge me on many levels. That's what makes it interesting.

2

Death and Nourishment

IN THE SPRING OF 1992, a young man named Christopher McCandless was learning how to hunt. His introduction to the act was not a gentle, gradual one. On the contrary, Christopher had been dropped off in the Alaskan wilderness with nothing more than a .22-caliber rifle, a sack of rice, a book on wild edible plants of the region and a collection of novels. He had embarked on a solitary pilgrimage into nature, hoping to eke out a livelihood for himself off the fat of the land. In fact, he had intentionally put himself into a position where he would *have* to successfully harvest plenty of food from the land, or go hungry trying.

For the first part of his expedition, Christopher had little luck hunting. He was unfamiliar with the land and inexperienced as a hunter. There was also little in the way of plant food available at the time, as the ground was still under snow. He thankfully had brought that sack of rice.

As the snow disappeared and the days quickly grew longer and warmer, his luck shifted and he began to have regular success hunting small animals. He shot and ate many squirrels, porcupines, ducks, grouse and other creatures, keeping a record of each one in his journal. In fact, the pages of his journal during that time did not really mention anything other than food; given his situation, its importance eclipsed all else.

His greatest success as a hunter came around the middle of June, when he managed to shoot and kill a cow moose. Although the animal was relatively modest in size (weighing probably between five and six hundred pounds), it still represented much more food than countless grouse and squirrels combined, and managing to kill it with a low-powered .22 caliber rifle (which is not a big enough gun to legally hunt even deer with) was a testament to his marksmanship. As anyone familiar with his story (and there are millions, as it was immortalized in the successful book and film *Into the Wild*) will know, however, McCandless' greatest moment as a hunter would also turn out to be one of the worst tragedies of his life.

Processing and preparing the small creatures that Christopher had been hunting was a simple affair. All he needed to do was skin, gut and cook them over the fire, perhaps keeping a bit of the meat cool for later by placing it in the shade with some ice from the river. A moose, however, is not a one-meal creature by any stretch, and because of its massive size presented a very different challenge. In the warm June temperatures, Christopher had only a limited amount of time to gut, skin, butcher and start preserving the meat before it would begin to degrade and become engulfed with maggots. Pulling this off by himself would have taken an enormous amount of energy and required a high level of skill and efficiency. That said, it's not rocket science, just hard work, and Christopher was clearly capable of that.

According to his journal, Christopher didn't actually gut the creature until the day after he had shot it, which would likely have given some of the meat a strong flavor, but in itself would not constitute a major disaster. When he did gut the animal, he removed the liver, kidneys and lungs and made a stew out of them, wanting to use the entire body of his kill.

As he was working on the carcass, he found the thick swarms of flies and mosquitoes descending on the raw flesh in the June heat unbearable. Eventually they forced him to work only in the cooler hours of nighttime. Slowly, he worked away, butchering the large carcass of the moose over several days.

Christopher had been told by some hunter friends down south that the best way to preserve meat in the bush is by smoking: hanging large sections of flesh over a low smoky fire, which alone would preserve it. Armed with this knowledge, he proceeded to work tirelessly for days building a makeshift smoker, maintaining a dull smoky fire within it and carefully suspending massive slabs of moose meat above the fire. Presumably he planned on curing the entire moose's meat in this way, but within a couple days of beginning his frantic effort, it was clear that this was not going to happen. Maggots quickly bloomed all over the meat, including the slabs and sections hanging in the improvised smoker, engulfing it in writhing masses. The weather, it seemed, was too hot for meat to be sitting out for days. But more troubling was the discovery that the advice he had been given on how to preserve all the meat turned out to be completely bogus. The thick slabs were not preserved at all.

Christopher, overwhelmed with grief, confusion and exhaustion, gave up at this point, abandoning the moose's carcass to the wolves. In his journal he wrote that killing that moose had been "one of the greatest tragedies of my life."

Inexperience and bad advice turned his successful hunt into a disaster. If Christopher had known how to effectively preserve meat under such conditions (by slicing it thin and hanging it to dry in the sun, not unlike drying laundry), or if he had known that he could actually take whole legs from that moose and bury them a couple feet deep in the earth to slowly age for months—if he had known any of these things he might have walked back to civilization in the fall and felt as though killing that moose was one of the most amazing things he had done in his life. But, in this story, he wasn't prepared.

He didn't come from a world that taught him any of these skills and had underestimated that handicap. And without those skills, Christopher starved to death later that summer.

This story, though an extremely sad one, illuminates many issues at the very heart of hunting.

The tragedy of it, the guilt that Christopher felt and wrote about in his journal, was not that he killed a cow moose. The tragedy was killing a cow moose and not being able to preserve it before it spoiled. He of course was not unique in this—countless others have identical secret stories and some even make a hobby out it—but his dramatic life and death have made his tale stand out.

What this scenario brings to light, among other things, is the quality that distinguishes hunting from any other act of basic killing: a hunter eats the body of the animal they have killed. Without this, all one is doing is killing. Unless they somehow make good use of their kill, what they have done is something that is seen almost universally as sad and tragic.

It could be said that what distinguishes hunting from senseless killing is the transformational cycle that surrounds the former: the death of the hunter's prey actually provides life to the hunter. The relationship between predator and prey is an alchemical one, where life energy crosses from one form to another. Indigenous cultures that live by hunting often have ceremonies and myths that reinforce this truism: that the hunter very literally *is* their prey, that they become so through this communion of death and nourishment. When a hunter fails to complete that cycle and eat what they have killed, as Christopher McCandless so tragically did in the spring of 1992 (and others do daily), all they are doing is taking a life. The carcass is never truly "wasted"; countless birds, beetles, maggots and microbes will devour and recycle it completely into the web of life. But the specific relationship between predator and prey, the transfer of life energy from one to the other, has not been fulfilled. This is why so many hunters feel called to "use it all" when they kill an animal—the more thoroughly they make use of their kill's body, the more complete that cycle is. One literally integrates the creature more fully into one's life (as well as those of family and friends) by doing this, making that transformation from death to nourishment.

Our culture, as a whole, doesn't really like to talk about this subject. It's one of the reasons so many people are uncomfortable with hunting: they're uncomfortable with death. But this cycle is not limited to the relationship between hunters and their prey. Hunting is just an unmistakable, in-your-face example of it. Really, it's the foundation of existence, and one of the most fascinating paradoxes of our lives: life feeds off of death. Without it, nothing alive would be able to exist. Whether you are a raw food vegan, a fast-food-eating slob or a full-blown paleo-diet carnivore, your food could not exist without death. The soil it comes from is itself a kind of decomposing transition zone where dead things are mixed up, broken down and reborn. Whether it is in the form of plants, insects, bacteria or mammals, any food we eat springs from the well of death. Which is to say that life, our lives, spring from the well of death. It's through a constant shifting of energy from death to life to death to life that the biological world hums along, which itself is a phenomenon that completely blurs the neat lines we'd like to draw between life and death.

Rebirth

If we were to make a list of the top five things that we as a society fear more than anything else, death would probably be around the top of it. Most other fears usually have death underlying them. If we made a list of the top five things that we as a society understand the least, death would likely be around the top of that one, also. One of the main reasons we fear death seems to be that we don't understand it, or to put it another way, because it is an unavoidable passageway to the unknown. The unknown is terrifying because we *can't* understand it. Despite all that science and civilization have determined about the nature of the universe, we still know almost nothing about one of the most significant and unavoidable aspects of existence: when we die, or when our friends, relatives and pets die, what happens to them? The part of them that is an aware, unique individual, the consciousness that filled their body, where does it go?

Hunting inevitably brings us into contact with these questions. Questions about mortality, about the mystery of death and about what it really is, that unseen force which animates a body, that makes one aware, awake, unique and alive—and can leave the body. When one kills a wild animal for food, seeing firsthand the mystery of death unfolding (and of course being completely responsible for it), there's a lot going on. Unfortunately, in the same way that most people have never gotten blood on their hands and experienced the carnal reality of their food, most people are not used to having something so basic, primal and mundane as eating come laced with this kind of depth.

As I mentioned earlier, when the hunter eats the animal they have killed, it becomes part of them. A death becomes a life; the predator and prey become one and the body of the dead, in a sense, lives on. This gets to something else that can be shaken through connecting with our food: our separation from the living world. When you kill and eat a creature, you are very literally integrating its body into yours. You are also integrating the land which that creature came from into your body, since their body was entirely a manifestation of that land. This is amazing, a dynamic that I think lies at the very heart of most people's desire to connect to the land, whether it be through gardening, hiking, foraging, crafting or hunting: shattering the boundary between self and other, human and nature; piercing the illusion of separation that in many ways defines our culture.

There are many practical reasons for people to take up foraging, hunting, gardening or other nature-based skills (health, sanity, economics, fun, etc.), but I believe that in most instances, in the modern world, any practical motive is accompanied or ultimately driven by this desire to *connect* and *integrate* with the living world around us, to step beyond duality; to *actually be part of nature*. As much as we might think we are looking for a different level of technology by pursuing these things, we're looking for a different level of consciousness; a different way of seeing and being in the world. Of course this different level of consciousness sounds very similar to what one might call compassion: to take away the boundaries that separate, numb and blind us from the feelings of others and allow ourselves to be open, connected, aware.

This is all part of the invisible soul food of the hunt, another kind of nourishment that it provides beyond the physical food. Of course, this soul food really doesn't exist without the physical, and isn't separate from it so much as it is a subtle aspect of it. In a world where we often think that meaningful experiences happen in places that are totally disconnected from grounded, day-to-day, physical reality, there is something refreshing about this.

Going back to Christopher McCandless and his moose hunt in the Alaskan wilderness: there is something about Christopher's unpreparedness that I and many others can in our own way relate to. Like him, we did not grow up in a culture that taught us the practical skills necessary to live gracefully on the land. Indeed, I have my own list of personal stories as a fumbling, bumbling hunter. These physical skills were not handed down to us, and we have never been guided through the complex emotional and energetic reality of these things. Interestingly, there might not be an enormous distinction between the two. When I ask the question, "*What could Christopher have been taught to prepare him, on an emotional or even spiritual level, for the gravity of killing that moose?*," the best answer I get is: "*How to quickly gut a creature and properly preserve its meat, fat, skin and organs.*"

You might feel that giving an offering, burning a smudge or saying a prayer is an important part of your hunting, but at the most fundamental level, simply making a swift kill and then making good use of the creature's body, fulfilling the cycle of death and nourishment, is the most direct way to honor any animal you have killed to eat.

And so the pages that follow are devoted to these practical skills, for the aspiring hunter, in hopes that you might approach your hunt prepared with the knowledge necessary to take and use the life of an animal in a respectful, reverent and humble way.

3

Studying Your Prey

WHEN I WAS SEVENTEEN I spent my first summer living alone in the woods, learning how to gather wild
edibles, grow a little vegetable garden and catch fish. A
few times a week I would go out in a little rowboat and jig for cod. I
had a rod, line, weights and lures and knew enough to tie everything
together, let my lure drop down to the ocean floor deep below me,
reel up a couple feet and then jig: yanking the rod up away from the

water's surface and then letting it fall back down at a slow, steady, rhythmic pace. Sometimes within a few minutes I would be reeling up a cod that would serve as much appreciated fresh protein.

Despite feeling extremely grateful for the fresh food, I also felt an unshakeable discomfort and sadness throughout the whole process of fishing. Every time I gutted a cod I couldn't help but think: *who am I to be killing this fish?* What made it feel so strange and uncomfortable was that I knew nothing about these cod I was killing. For lack of a better word, I felt that I was essentially an alien dropping a line into some unknown depth, an unseen dimension, and pulling out a living thing I really didn't understand at all, so that I could kill it. I felt disconnected. I never reconciled this dilemma that summer, and even decided to not fish again for a couple years afterward. Over time, however, I realized that it wasn't really what I was doing that didn't feel good, it was my *lack of understanding* of the realm I was entering and feeding from. It was my ignorance. To really feel comfortable killing something for my food, I realized that I needed to understand what it was I was killing, needed to come to the process with a level of awareness and humility. The more I understood about my prey, the less I felt like a clueless tourist and the more sane everything felt.

On a practical level, studying your prey is the prerequisite to pursuing it in an intelligent, confident way. The more you know about its habits, seasonal rhythms, food sources, signs, biology, senses and sensitivities, the better a hunter you will be. The more time you spend in the woods, meadows or clearings that your prey calls home, scouting out potential hunting grounds and getting familiar with them, the more you will learn.

The particular traits, behaviors and other facets of one's prey that a hunter could potentially study are almost inexhaustible; here I will touch on just a few of the most obvious ones. They include the basics of learning how to recognize and read the tracks and sign of your prey; having a basic understanding of the anatomy, biology and seasonal rhythms it lives by; understanding its senses and sensitivities;

and being familiar with the ecology your prey calls home. Whatever your quarry, these areas of knowledge will help you approach it more effectively.

A focus on deer

To go into the behavior, biology, tracks, sign and hunting technique involved with even some of the potential creatures one might choose to hunt for food is beyond the scope of this book. Because of this, I will use deer as a general reference animal here and throughout the following chapters, branching into relevant information about other animals here and there when it is called for. I have chosen deer as a keystone because the various species of deer are extremely widespread and wherever they roam, represent perhaps the ideal animal for the subsistence hunter. The amount of nourishment that comes out of one adult deer is quite substantial, and they are quarry that people who live in less wild areas and cannot afford to go on hunting expeditions in search of moose or caribou can still realistically harvest. I harvested deer for years without owning a vehicle, without much in the way of money and without traveling any great distances. I did have the luxury of living close to large areas of forest, but such areas are reasonably accessible to many people.

A black-tailed deer doe munching on fireweed.

Deer are truly one of the archetypal prey animals. In old English, the word *deer* itself originally meant a wild animal of any kind. Over time this was narrowed down to one archetypal wild animal: deer. This is likely because they are so substantial to the hunter, and so widespread across many far-flung landscapes and cultural regions.

While the habits and attributes of deer vary between the various species, and other prey animals have very different behavior and biology, looking into the areas of knowledge that are relevant to the deer hunter will be instructive in showing what kind of understanding, information and awareness one should come to any hunt armed with.

Species

There are several distinct species of deer in North America, each of which inhabit different landscapes and have slight variations in behavior and biology. There are many overarching commonalities between these species, but you will want to familiarize yourself with the particular species of deer native to the area you'll be hunting.

White-tailed deer have the largest range of North American deer, mule deer (the largest species in the Americas) inhabit a smaller range, and black-tailed deer are found along the western coast of North America from northern California up into Alaska. Where black-tailed deer and mule deer territory overlaps, the two species may interbreed, creating a kind of transition zone of hybrid deer.

Some of the superficial distinctions between these three species of deer are that whitetails have the trademark white tail and antlers that do not branch, sending tines up out of a central stalk. Mule deer have a black-tipped tail, large ears (like a mule's) and branching antlers. Black-tailed deer, the smallest of the continental American deer, have distinctive black tails and antlers that are branched and typically smaller than the other species.

Habitat

Deer can be found in many landscapes and travel throughout various terrain regularly, often gravitating to transition zones between one ecology and another. The varied ecology they roam through provide deer with a range of food as well as cover/protection. The greatest concentration of deer and general animal activity are often found in ecological *edges*.

Where deer are found depends on two main factors: available food sources and pressure from predators. This is why deer populations often skyrocket in agricultural and suburban areas: the amount of forage is greatly increased by human influence on the land, while human predation is restricted and non-human predation is often eliminated. Human-created clearings, whether the result of logging, suburban sprawl, farming or other activity, can all contribute to elevated deer population. Deer live in such diverse areas that it is impossible to simplify their potential habitat. If you live in the wilderness of the Rocky Mountains or a highly agricultural landscape dotted with just small patches of forest, you'll be looking at two extremely diverse potential deer habitats.

It is this adaptability, the fact that deer can thrive in varied and changing environments, that makes them so resilient.

Resilience

In the late 1800s, deer were hunted to near extinction in many parts of North America. An insatiable demand for meat and hides created a booming, unregulated backwoods industry of market hunting. With no protection from market hunters, American deer populations had declined to less than five hundred thousand by the beginning of the 20th century. To put this number into context, five hundred thousand is less than half of the present-day deer population in the state of Pennsylvania. In the early 1900s, one of the first real pieces of wildlife conservation legislation, the Lacey Act, was passed with the specific intention of protecting deer populations. It worked; as the pressure of market hunting eased, deer populations rebounded quickly and today are extremely robust across most of North America, to the point that many wildlife biologists consider deer overpopulation a serious problem in many areas.

It is worth noting that, during this same period of time, the American bison was also hunted to near extinction. Although bison are now beginning to make a comeback, they have not recovered in the same way as deer have by a long shot. Deer, given the same pressure and intensity of market slaughter, were able to make a much more dramatic and rapid recovery. This is probably largely due to their inherent adaptability. Capable of living in a diverse range of ecological niches and able to evade predation by taking to more protective terrain, deer are *extremely* resilient.

Bison, on the other hand, occupy more open terrain in larger groups, which would have made them in some ways easier prey for old time market hunters. It also limited their ability to rebound once that pressure was reduced, as their large traditional ranges were increasingly developed by settlers. Where the bison's ecological needs are a bit more specific, it is the extreme adaptability of deer that has allowed them to rebound and thrive so robustly.

Biology of deer

Deer are hoofed herbivores, members of the ungulate group of mammals that have multiple chambered stomachs for slowly fermenting and digesting plants. Their main predators in the wild are large carnivores such as wolves and cougars, although many other creatures will prey on the sick, injured and old. In areas where such predators are scarce or non-existent, humans and human activity generally represent deer's main source of predation (in the forms of habitat destruction, automobile-inflicted fatalities and hunting).

Deer are most active during the twilight hours of dusk and dawn. They can also be quite active during the nighttime hours, and during the summer and fall will often be seen out in the open during the middle of the day. So it is impossible to say there is any time deer really can't be active, but it is true to say that they are *most* active at dusk and dawn.

In areas where pressure from predators (human or non-human) is significant, deer will tend toward a more nocturnal schedule.

Digestion

Deer are strict herbivores and are classified as ruminant mammals. This means that they are "cud chewers" with a multiple-chambered stomach that slowly digests plant material through a process of bacterial fermentation, regurgitation, chewing and further digestion. When deer are out feeding on vegetation, what they are really doing is more akin to collecting food in a container (a chamber of their stomach, in this case) where they can store it and begin breaking it down for eating later. When they are at rest, bedded down, deer regurgitate this stored food and chew it properly. This is when they really eat their food. For a prey animal that wants to spend as little time exposed and vulnerable to predation as possible, this is a brilliant adaptation, allowing them to continue feeding while resting someplace protected and safe.

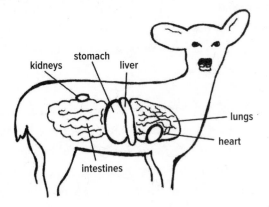

The internal anatomy of a deer, showing various organs.

The process of fermentation that occurs in the deer's stomachs (rumen) allows it to eat a wide range of foods. The cultures present in their rumen actually evolve and shift to accommodate various kinds of forage. If, for example, a deer has been feeding primarily on tender vegetation, and suddenly the weather changes, say a couple feet of snow fall and all that is available is woody browse, the deer's gut will take several days to adjust while entirely different cultures develop to ferment and digest the new and different food.

A deer's mouth lacks upper incisors (the big, sharp front teeth that you show when you smile), having a toothless pad where these would otherwise be. They do have lower incisors, though, which they use to grip and tear vegetation with. This is why a branch or sapling that a deer has fed on will sometimes look more torn than cleanly chomped.

Seasonal rhythms

Birth: Deer mate in the fall, and after a gestation period of about seven months, give birth the following year during mid-late spring/early summer. A doe has one or two fawns (this depending largely on age and food supply), who for the next two to three months will nurse and learn some of the basics of being a deer. Fawns are born with white spots on their coat that serve as a simple camouflage. They are able to walk within hours of birth and typically begin eating solid food just a few days after being born.

In the fall fawns lose the white spots on their coat and are weaned from their mother's milk.

Coat: In the spring, as temperatures rise, deer shed their thick, luscious winter coats, a phase that often gives them a ragged, moth-eaten look. The summer coat is typically lighter in color and thinner. In the fall, as weather cools, the coat thickens and changes color slightly again, taking on a more lustrous sheen.

Antlers: All male North American deer grow and shed a new set of antlers every year. A buck's antlers represent an enormous amount of energy: as much minerals and nutrients go into their development as it takes for a doe to produce a fully developed fetus. The antlers emerge in the spring, when they are covered in a spongy, fuzzy tissue referred to as *velvet*. They then grow rapidly during the summer months. In late summer or early fall, as soon as their antlers have reached their full size, the bucks scrape off the outer sheath of velvet, typically by vigorously rubbing their antlers against trees. This antler velvet is an esteemed medicine in many cultures, used as a strengthening virility tonic. Some bucks eat the fresh velvet once they have scraped it off, probably to get the medicinal benefits for themselves. By then the antlers are fully formed dense bone whose main purpose is the role they play in the annual drama of sex and power. During the summer and early fall, bucks playfully spar with each other, bashing their racks together, which produces a wonderful clicking sound. As mating season draws nearer, these "friendly" sparring matches get less and less amicable. Eventually they transform into harsh, potentially lethal battles for dominance of an area or female courtship. As mating season approaches, bucks also begin vigorously rubbing their antlers against trees and saplings, strengthening their necks, which will become swollen and enlarged during the rut, in preparation for any such battles.

After the rut has passed and winter closes in fully, bucks shed their antlers and stop beating each other up.

Mating: The annual mating season occurs in the late fall, usually sometime between October and December. During the rut deer behaviors change considerably. Bucks that spend much of the rest of the year happily fraternizing with other bucks now become aggressive toward one another in hopes of establishing dominance and, well, getting laid. Many are so completely preoccupied with mating that their feeding patterns become sporadic for a period during the peak of the rut.

Does are likewise preoccupied with mating during this period. They only go into estrus (ovulation) for 24 to 48 hours, but during this time they may mate with one or more bucks several times. If they didn't mate or get pregnant during that first ovulation, they will ovulate a second time about a month later and mate again. After this second window, the winter settles in and there won't be any more action until the following year.

Deer communicate with each other a great deal during this time, notably through a means that we cannot see or detect: scent. Through urine and the excretions of external glands, deer are capable of sending and receiving a great deal of information to help them find that much sought after moment of intimacy.

After the rut ends and winter descends in full, bucks go their own way and return to bachelor life, having nothing further to do with the doe or their offspring.

Daily rhythms

As mentioned earlier, deer are generally most active at dusk and dawn. Though they aren't nocturnal, they can choose to feed and mingle under the safety of darkness. Often deer will bed down during the middle of the day, which may involve sleeping, but also gives them an important opportunity to slowly chew their cud.

Sensory awareness

Deer really are an archetype for sensitivity. With their big ears listening for the quietest noise, their eyes scanning for the slightest movement and capable of seeing in very low light, and their noses able to pick up the slightest scent at a level that would be absolutely inconceivable to us, deer are tuned in and aware of even slight disturbances in the environment.

Sound

The large ears of deer gather and funnel sound from the environment, providing effective protection from danger. Muscles around the base of their ears allow them to swivel forward and backward, to focus on the direction from which any sound is coming. A particularly clumsy footstep is sometimes all it takes to spook a deer and send it bounding into the distance.

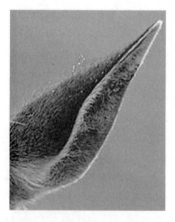

A deer's ears function like natural funnels, collecting sound from the environment.

Besides constantly listening for any sound that is out of the ordinary and could signal danger, deer are also attentive to the sounds of other creatures. Birds, squirrels and other creatures will often go quiet or make alarming noises when something is out of the ordinary. Deer can pick up on these subtleties, which provide a kind of secondary alert system.

Sight

The location of a deer's eyes on the sides of its head gives it a very wide field of vision. Deer can see 300 degrees around, making them highly aware of their surroundings. They are not actually able to focus with both eyes on the same point at the same time (as you are doing while reading this), but, rather, are constantly surveying a broad field of vision. This is very effective with regards to sensing any danger on the horizon.

Deer also have strong night vision which allows them to be fully aware of their surroundings during the dull and dark hours of dusk, night and dawn.

Though their daytime vision is not so strong as their night vision, it is still pretty sharp. They do however have poor depth perception, because both eyes can't focus on the same area at the same time, and see at a lower resolution than humans. Deer also do not register as broad a spectrum of color as humans.

Despite these shortcomings, deer still have eyesight that is pretty strong, being panoramic and capable of picking up subtle movements, if not colors or depths. This is why it is so important to master stillness when deer hunting.

Smell

Smell is probably the deer's sharpest sense. A deer receives a great deal of information in the form of scents that may be imperceptible to us. Their keen sense of smell allows them to detect danger as well as communicate among one another.

Understanding their powerful ability to pick up subtle, imperceptible odors, many hunters prepare for hunting by doing whatever they can to reduce or eliminate their own scent.

Thimbleberry bushes that have been visited by foraging deer. Note that many of the top stems have had their leaves chomped off.

Food

The diet of deer can vary quite a bit, depending on the local ecology and what is seasonally available. For example, whitetails in the acorn-bearing forests of the eastern states have a very different diet than mule deer in the rocky mountains. Still, there are many commonalities in the diets of all North American deer.

Deer typically forage much of their diet as browsers ("browse" refers to twigs, leaves, buds and other tough or woody plant material), feeding also on tender grasses and forbs (tender, herbaceous plants), seeds, fungi and fruits (such as wild berries), in season.

During the warm moist months of spring and summer, the diet will often be composed of more tender vegetation. In the winter, deer may subsist solely on woody browse, lichen and whatever other vegetation is not beneath snow, although they will dig in snow for some foods.

Social organization

Throughout most of the year, bucks congregate in what are known as bachelor groups, which are essentially rowdy all-boys clubs. Does spend much of the year in family units, comprised of numerous does along with any fawns or yearlings they might be rearing. Yearling fawns will usually be kicked out of these groups some time after they reach a year in age, at which point they will travel and hook up with a bachelor group (if they're male) or a new family unit (if they're female). Sometimes adult bucks can be seen amid one of these maternal groups, but it is not the norm.

Within both buck and doe groups, one individual typically emerges as the dominant figure. A dominant doe will usually be the first in the group to mate during the rut, choosing her favorite buck ahead of all the others. She will also have dibs on the best fawning area. A dominant buck will likewise assert his power and dominance during mating season.

During the autumn rut these normally segregated populations intermingle, because does are suddenly more interested in being around bucks and vice versa. All kinds of interesting drama results (more on this later).

Tracks and sign

Knowing how to recognize common animal tracks or pick up the trail of a creature and follow it are basic skills any hunter will become acquainted with. The tracks animals leave on soft spots in the forest floor, in meadows, along creek beds or elsewhere are valuable sources of information. They speak a language that, once one begins to learn it even at a rudimentary level, reveal clues that can be precious to a hunter.

There are schools of outdoors enthusiasts that have refined tracking to a precise science. Tom Brown Jr.'s method of "pressure release" tracking falls into this realm. By carefully studying the depth, spacing, weight distribution and other minute but measurable attributes of tracks, Brown has apparently deciphered how to read not just information like approximately when the tracks were left or which way the animal turned when the trail seems to disappear, but other very precise details like if it had to pee, if it was hungry, if it was full, if it was horny, if it was in a bit of a hurry, etc. I think this is amazing, but personally have found that a much more basic, commonsense understanding of tracks and tracking has been sufficient for my simple subsistence hunting needs.

That said, even a very basic understanding of tracks and tracking can transform one's experience of a walk in the woods. There is a story being told by tracks. Perhaps the story is as simple as seeing that a large, solitary deer was walking the path you are on after it stopped raining early this morning, as the tracks are completely crisp and have not been eroded at all by rainfall. The track pattern of this solitary deer shows that it seems to have stopped several times while it was walking, and when you look around to see why, you see where it chomped on some leaves alongside the trail. Under certain

Deer tracks. When running or walking on soft ground, the dewclaws will show and the hooves will sometimes spread apart, as shown in the track on the right.

A typical deer track pattern.

conditions, tracks can tell the story of an area's recent history in a readable way.

By tuning into this information one can get an idea of who calls a given area home, how active different populations are within it, *what the patterns of those creatures are* and other information that will determine good spots to hunt. One can also use tracks to directly stalk prey, or to pursue it after a shot.

When tracking, one of course does not rely solely on footprints. Pushed-down vegetation, broken branches and other visible disturbances allow one to trail an animal when its tracks are not present or disappear. Some environments do not lend themselves to easy tracking as there is either no soft ground for tracks to register in or they are covered in dense, hardy vegetation.

Reading a track

Some information is directly apparent in any series of tracks. To start, one can determine, at least approximately, how fresh it is. The biggest clues come from observing how weather has degraded it. A track that is less than 24 hours old in clear weather will usually maintain a crisp, clean look, with good definition around its edges. It will usually also be free of any debris. As tracks age, that sharpness erodes. During rainy weather this ageing is sped up considerably. During freezing weather, sometimes one can tell a very fresh track by looking closely and seeing if frost crystals have formed inside it. If not, you may be literally hot on the trail of a creature. When you find such fresh tracks, look around and switch your stealth on, as whoever left the track could very well be nearby.

If you are out scouting for potential hunting spots, it is less important how fresh the tracks you find are (unless they are clearly *really* old) and more important to get a sense of the general patterns of your prey there. Here are some tips for reading deer tracks:

- If you are following a series of tracks and see that the deer was making frequent stops, it's possible that it was feeding. Look around whenever you see it paused to see if this was the case.

- When a deer is moving steadily along a trail and suddenly veers off into thick bush, this can sometimes indicate that it was heading to bed down. It can really push one's senses to head into more brushy terrain and attempt to follow a deer's course. Take note of any likely bedding sites; knowing where they are can be helpful in understanding a deer's movement patterns.
- Try to determine where a set of tracks are going. What is the purpose of the deer's movement? Is it going to feed? If so, on what, and where? Push yourself to try and understand.

These suggestions for reading tracks are really just examples of common sense. For a person who has spent their life in a city or the suburbs, this may be a kind of *uncommon* common sense, but a lot of tracking is as simple as paying attention, tuning in and looking for the story. The more time one spends walking the woods, meadows, field edges and other areas paying attention to these subtle details, the more attuned one will become to reading tracks and putting together that story. Walking the same area daily in the rainy season will show you how rain degrades the tracks there as you observe fresh tracks appear and fade. Walking it in the summer will show the less perceptible effects of wind and heat.

This is really the best way to learn how to read tracks and study your prey: spending time outdoors and paying attention. The more time you spend there, the more you will notice. And the more you hunt, the more this knowledge will become applied and experiential.

To be an effective subsistence hunter you don't need to become a master tracker. In fact the tracking skills required are pretty basic, but you may well find yourself enchanted by and drawn deeply into the language and art of it. Many philosophers believe that the limits of one's language are the limits of one's world. The language we speak, think and receive information in shapes our reality in profound ways. It is a filter through which we perceive life, and as such, a filter that limits our understanding of it. I've referred to *the language* of tracks a few times already, and do believe that there is

Deer trail.

a language which they speak. The more one becomes fluent in such languages of the land, the more expansive the reality they live in becomes. The forests and fields grow more alive and intense as we pay closer attention.

Trails

Many creatures travel in predictable patterns, on established trails and runs that are easily spotted within their territory. Deer are an excellent example of this, forging extensive, easily distinguishable networks of trails throughout forests and clearings. Deer trails look like scaled-down human trails and are typically very easy to spot and follow. Some trails are what I like to call highways—well-traveled thoroughfares—whereas others might only be occasionally used. Studying a trail for sign should indicate the general amount of use.

A well-worn deer thoroughfare coursing through a wooded area or a spot where many trails congregate at the edge of a clearing is an active artery of deer movement. When scouting out areas for hunting, it is these veins and arteries that one naturally gravitates toward in search of information. You may want to set up to hunt within comfortable shooting range of places like these, or otherwise plan a hunt around them.

Think like your prey

Another tool in the tracker's toolkit (and again, this might just sound like common sense) is trying to think like whoever it is you are tracking. This process can be both logical and intuitive. By understanding your prey's behavior and biology you can imagine what it might be thinking. When you lose its trail you can imagine what it was thinking and see if this produces any hints. The more you know about your prey, the more this can develop. It relies mainly on logic.

Many trackers also rely heavily on intuition to guide them as they follow a creature's trail, but I should emphasize that even if you are using your "sixth sense," there are five other preceding senses that must be kept sharp and attuned to track effectively. Without a solid foundation in the physical, relying on intuition is ungrounded. Literally.

Some scoff at giving credence to gut feelings or any kind of intuitive guidance as a tracking tool, but I have had personal experiences and know numerous hunters who would not have recovered kills had they not had their "antennae" open and receptive to subtle nudges of intuition. Indeed, many hunters consider intuition to be vital to their effectiveness. To put it simply: when you are tracking, let yourself be open and receptive. One has to embody this to some extent to track at all; to catch subtleties that require sharp awareness and attention to be seen. But it can be helpful to loosen the mind's normally narrow vision a little bit more.

In most cases, there is already plenty of physical information for the tracker to try and understand, follow or learn from.

Sign

As I mentioned earlier, you shouldn't rely on tracks alone when tracking. The woods are full of information in other forms of sign.

Aside from tracks and trails, there is a plethora of other sign one can look for to determine how active any given species is in an area, what kind of activity occurs there (travel, feeding, bedding, mating, etc.) and much more. Below are a few of these kinds of sign.

Droppings

Droppings probably come in next to tracks on the list of basic animal sign. Like tracks, droppings provide plenty of valuable information.

There is no real science to telling if droppings are fresh. The visual cues are clear and obvious: fresh poo just looks fresh. It has an almost glossy sheen to it; a slight moistness on its exterior. During dry weather, this sheen will disappear after a day as it begins to dry on the outside. After several days, the process of drying will have proceeded in a very clear way. Eventually, if the weather is dry the dropping will become pale, dry and crumbly. You don't need to pick up a deer turd and smush it between your fingers to determine this, although it might be fun, and if it is still warm you will know it is *really* fresh.

What can a pile of deer droppings tell you?

- *The texture and shape of droppings can indicate what a creature has been eating.* When one stumbles upon a pile of deer droppings, its shape can give a clue as to what the deer was feeding on. Round, individual pellets indicate that a deer has been eating tougher, drier vegetation (hardy leaves, woody browse, etc.). Droppings that are clumped together indicate a diet of more tender vegetation (grasses and forbs).

Clumped deer droppings.   Pellet-shaped deer droppings.

- *The number of droppings in an area gives you clues about how many creatures live there.* At the simplest level, a lot of fresh droppings in an area tell you it's currently active.
- *The location of droppings can give clues about feeding and bedding.* Like humans, many creatures feel the greatest urge to poo at predictable times: upon waking up and after eating a big meal. Although this isn't always the case, sometimes when you find many droppings clustered together, suggesting a frequently used poop spot, it can indicate that a frequently visited bedding or feeding site is nearby.
- *Picking apart a creature's stool can reveal what it's been eating.* Before I say anything else about this, let me give a warning: Don't try this with all creatures' droppings. The poo of raccoons, cats and other omnivorous or carnivorous creatures should not be picked up and played with casually. This is because these creatures can be host to a number of parasites that have reportedly made humans very sick, and these parasites are shed or spread through feces. Even inhaling spores that are emitted from raccoon dung is potentially dangerous. So as a rule, avoid holding the crap of meat-eating creatures in your bare hands. Herbivore poop, on the other hand, is generally quite safe to handle.

  There is no great secret to dissecting a pellet or turd to see what a creature has been eating; simply break it apart and see what you see. One can have a lot of fun looking at the digested remains of various plants and figuring out what they were.

One of last fall's antler rubs found during late summer scouting. Several small saplings in this area had been completely de-barked and died as a result of vigorous antler rubbing.

Beds

A deer bed is typically an oval-shaped impression or disturbance made into debris on a forest floor, grass, other vegetation or snow. Often deer will select bedding sites in dense brush, up high or wherever else provides the greatest protection from predators. The more pressure a deer is under from predation, the more effort it will put into bedding down someplace safe and sound. Conversely, in some suburban areas that deer call home, there is no real pressure from predators so it's no surprise to see a deer bedded down on someone's front lawn in the middle of the day, chewing its cud.

Much of the time a deer passes bedded down is dedicated to regurgitating and chewing small amounts of food. Deer spend many hours each day like this, bedded down chewing cud, "ruminating" in silence.

Knowing the general area where your prey rests in this way can be helpful in establishing its patterns, as one of the most predictable patterns it will have is regularly traveling between bedding sites and feeding areas. Deer can have many bedding sites and sometimes shuffle between them as a clever strategy to elude predation. Still, many deer will bed in the same general area if not the same spot regularly, and knowing where that is can help you establish their travel patterns.

Rubs

Beginning at the end of the summer and into the fall, bucks remove the velvet coating on their antlers by rubbing them against tree trunks. This rubbing also wounds the tree, scraping bark off and leaving a permanent scar. Sometimes small saplings are even killed when a buck removes too much of their bark. After removing this velvet, bucks continue this vigorous rubbing against the trunks of trees and saplings throughout the fall, to strengthen their necks for potential sparring and sharpen their antlers. A buck will often come back to and use the same rub repeatedly. Fresh rubs are clear, valuable sign of buck activity in an area, while old ones show how much activity there has been in the last year or previous years.

4

Tools

IN THIS DAY AND AGE, the choice to hunt our own food forces us to step out of the hi-tech, fast-paced modern reality and into a slower, subtler connection to a completely different reality: the natural world. This process can give the hunter an interesting viewpoint on our culture's disconnection from nature and how technology has the power to alienate us from nature, each other and ourselves. Most people cannot experience the juxtaposition of patiently harvesting wild meat from the earth and sitting in a traffic jam without having some quiet revelations about humanity, nature and technology.

Because hunting almost by design stirs up thoughts and questions about our connection to or disconnection from nature, any discussion about the tools one chooses to execute it with, then, should be prefaced with a few comments on this disconnect.

Tools, technology and connection

Without tools, we can't hunt. Lacking the physical attributes of creatures like wolves, cats, hawks and other predators (sharp claws or talons, for example), without the help of some very basic tools, the human hunter is limited to small prey (eaten whole and uncooked), insects and plant foods. Some of the very first simple tools that early humans developed were wooden spears with fire-hardened tips, throwing sticks, clubs and flakes of stone used for cutting through skin and flesh. The rise of tool-making allowed early humans to progress as hunters. The new tools and hunting techniques opened countless doors, including the door to new lands that had previously been uninhabitable, the door to new ways of relating to the earth and each other and the door, eventually, to here and now.

One of the most interesting things about any technology is that at the same time as it opens many doors, it can close many others. Every succeeding level of technology gives its user more power, more control, more efficiency (for example: the progression from wooden bow to high-powered rifle with a quality scope set on a stand), but with each incremental jump in power, we have less direct connection to whatever it is we are trying to accomplish.

But this is the point, right? Less work, more efficiency.

Well, yes and no. It really depends on what your goal is.

If you are cutting a tree down with stone tools (something I have never done, and don't particularly want to do), you will have a certain type of connection with that tree and the process of taking its life. You will at the very least notice that individual tree, for it will take you some time to cut it down. After spending so much time with it, you will surely feel a kind of appreciation and admiration for it, and even remember it in the future.

If you cut down a tree with an ax or handsaw, this connection will change slightly. If you use a chainsaw, it will change some more, as the faller will now only have to spend a moment with the tree before it comes crashing down. If you use a modern feller-buncher, you will not really notice that individual tree at all, as it is cut and bunched so rapidly, along with many other trees.

With each increase in control and efficiency, we have less time for connection, less of a relationship and consequently less understanding. When our lives veer too far in the direction of a fully automated, mechanized reality, we risk losing our entire connection to the basic, fundamental forces that guide life. These are the forces that help us understand ourselves. If your goal is strictly cold, prosaic efficiency, that loss of connection and understanding doesn't matter. If your goal, however, is precisely that lost connection and understanding, well then, this is something to think about. Most hunters (and people) are looking for a balance between these two polarities. You really wouldn't bother hunting at all unless you wanted to personally find this balance. It would be far more efficient, after all, to just go get some burgers at the drive-through.

What does this have to do with hunting tools? As I already mentioned, hunting connects us directly to nature and our source of nourishment, and there is a range of tools we can use, each with different merits and drawbacks. A high-powered rifle with a good scope is more powerful and easier to gain confidence with than a wooden longbow. A longbow requires much more practice to master, has a much more limited effective range and so demands much more prowess to use, but for those who are attracted to those very features, it can be considered part of a process that connects the hunter to the hunt. Like the stone tools and the chainsaw, both have their merits and their drawbacks.

I don't personally think there is any morally superior method of hunting. We all choose what weapon we will hunt with based on what is practical within our life, what is effective and economically feasible, what we feel confident and capable with, etc. Being comfortable and capable with your weapon of choice is the most important thing, as this is what will determine your ability to make a clean kill.

What follows is a brief discussion of the merits and drawbacks of different hunting tools, as well as information on a number of other basic tools necessary for any hunting, from modern high-powered rifles to handmade wooden bows. Your choice of a tool may be determined in part by where you want to hunt. Your local hunting regulations will specify what areas are shotgun- or bow-only zones, or where rifles are allowed.

Whatever tool you choose, there will be many books on its proper use and care, as well as online resources, local courses, clubs and staff at sporting shops. All these sources can also help you find the right gun, bow or what have you, and teach you how to shoot.

The hunting knife

Before getting into the realm of guns and bows, it makes sense to mention one of the most important tools of any hunter: a knife. Without this simple piece of equipment, one can't begin any of the real work that immediately follows making a kill (gutting, skinning, basic butchering). There is a temptation among beginning (and some experienced) hunters to arm themselves with a macho knife: an enormous blade that could double as a small sword. For simple hunting uses, such jumbo blades are both unnecessary and often impractical. An eight-inch-long blade looks impressive and is ideal for chopping firewood, but for gutting a squirrel or a deer it is actually quite cumbersome. The big blade is too large and lanky to work gracefully in narrow spaces. A simple, sturdy knife with a three- to four-inch blade is all one actually needs to completely process most North American deer. For larger animals, the same size of knife can work, and a saw is often used as well to cut through bone.

Folding blades

Knives with folding blades have a very clear advantage over those with fixed blades: they are more compact. They can be stored without a sheath, and so are more casual and unobtrusive to carry. There are many folding-type knives that are both affordable and high quality.

The big drawbacks to a folding blade are: the locking mechanism that holds the blade in place can fail during hard work, allowing the blade to unexpectedly and dangerously fold closed on your fingers (not fun!); the little nooks of the folding knife are great places for gunk (meat, blood) to collect (not the end of the world, but not something that happens with a fixed blade).

Despite all of this, many hunters still prefer folding knives. The main thing to keep in mind when selecting such a knife is the locking mechanism—lots of cheap folding knives have mechanisms that are dangerously inadequate for any real work. Make sure any knife you use has a strong, solid lock that won't budge under pressure.

Fixed blades

Fixed-blade knives are a bit more cumbersome to carry, but worth the extra volume. The most practical blade size for a hunting knife probably lies between three and a half and five inches long. A fixed blade is safer to use than a folding knife, as it doesn't rely on a fickle locking mechanism to keep the blade from folding in on the user's fingers.

Stainless versus carbon steel

Knives come in many different grades of steel, but these can be boiled down to the distinction between stainless steel and carbon steel. Without going into the science, the simplest way to describe the difference is that stainless steel will not rust easily and is harder, which makes it harder to sharpen. Once a stainless steel knife begins to seriously lose its edge, it can take some serious TLC to get it back.

Carbon steel will rust if it is left wet for too long (which can be remedied using a wire brush). Most kinds of carbon steel will lose an edge faster than stainless steel, but are also generally easier to re-sharpen. The ease with which a carbon steel blade can be touched up to extreme sharpness makes it a preferred choice for many.

I use stainless and carbon steel knives interchangeably when hunting. I like carbon for the ease with which it can be touched up, but also do have to take a wire brush to it every once in a while.

Rifles

Rifles are likely the most common hunting tool in use today. Their effective range, power and ease of use make them the obvious tool of choice for many. If your life doesn't accommodate the time and dedication required to master the art of shooting a bow, for instance, and you simply want to harvest your own meat in the most precise and humane way, a rifle is often the best option.

The word *rifle* has its root in the *rifling* on the inside of a gun's barrel. This is a pattern of spiralling grooves cut into the inner walls of the barrel that impart a spin to the bullet being fired. This spin effect gives a bullet leaving the barrel an aerodynamic stability that greatly improves range and accuracy. Archers have known about this principal for ages—the feathers used for natural arrow fletchings have a natural curvature that creates this same spinning effect when an arrow is shot. Football players also take advantage of this phenomena, giving a slight spin to the ball when they throw it to help stabilize its flight.

The effective range that rifles have over other hunting weapons makes them unsafe to use in certain areas. "Shotgun only" areas, which often also allow the use of bows, are designated zones where hunting is permitted, but because of nearby human activity, rifles are not allowed due to the risks of stray bullets. This would be one drawback of the rifle.

Choosing a rifle

There is no one rifle that is considered an all-purpose hunting gun. Certain cartridges are used for small animals, while others are suited to deer-sized animals or larger, and within these distinctions there are countless options. For hunting small animals (rabbit, squirrel, grouse, etc.), the .22 long rifle is often considered the quintessential firearm. The ammo is cheap (five hundred rounds usually cost about twenty bucks—compared to higher-powered cartridges that may cost over a dollar a round, that's really economical!) and it's a quiet gun with no recoil, making it extremely pleasant and easy to master. For hunting "big game" animals, however, one must use a higher-powered cartridge.

When choosing a deer rifle, for instance, a major consideration is the balance between two things: power and recoil. The recoil or "kickback" of certain calibers can make them difficult for some to shoot comfortably or effectively. This depends somewhat on the physiology of the shooter.

The .270 is a common deer cartridge that combines a great deal of power with minimal recoil. Other common deer cartridges are the .308 and .30/06, both of which also combine high power with minimal recoil. Higher-powered cartridges like the .338 are often used for hunting larger animals like elk and moose. Given all this differentiation, most hunters that use rifles tend to own more than one.

Aside from finding the appropriate caliber, you will also want to choose a style and size of gun that feels comfortable to use, as well as the action (the mechanism you "cock" to reload the gun) that feels most natural. You can find out much more about all of the fine details of choosing the right gun, the right scope and the right ammo from the countless resources available on this subject (which include, as mentioned earlier, your local outdoor sports store, research online or in books about firearms). Here I have only touched on the very basics.

Outfitted with a good scope that has been sighted in properly, rifles are the most effective long-range hunting tool.

Shotgun

The shotgun is probably the second most common modern hunting tool. Its name comes from the fact that instead of firing a single projectile, as a rifle does, a shotgun can often be used to fire shells loaded with a number of projectiles or a spray of metal pellets called shot. Shotgun shells can also be loaded with slugs, which are single, solid projectiles. These burly little things fully deserve the name slug, as anyone who has shot them will know. They have greater power, range and accuracy than the various types of shot.

Birdshot and buckshot

When firing shot, a shotgun is handled quite differently than a rifle. Instead of being outfitted with scopes and sighted in to achieve dead-on accuracy, a shooter typically relies on a simple metal bead at the end of the gun's barrel as their sight, and shoots more instinctively, at close range and often at moving or flying targets.

Shotgun shells are loaded with different sizes or kinds of shot for different kinds of hunting. *Birdshot*, for instance, is loaded with small metal projectiles that are shot or sprayed out into a broad swath; in many cases these are lead pellets, which is bad news for the land that gets sprayed with them, not to mention the food they are sprayed into! (Non-toxic steel shot is becoming more common, and is now actually legally required in many areas.) This obviously requires much less precision on the part of the shooter. It also requires that one shoot at close range, as the spray pattern grows wider with distance and the pellets lose their velocity quickly. Using different chokes and shot sizes will produce a different shot pattern and effective range. Bird shot is used for hunting waterfowl and other small game at close range.

Buckshot is loaded with much larger projectiles/shot, and is somewhat controversial. It is used by many for deer hunting, hence the name, while others insist that it is unethical as it can cripple deer without killing them. This is because the shot is fired in a spray-like pattern and cannot strike with the precision of a single projectile. Properly patterned with the correct choke and at close range (generally 35 yards or less), buckshot can be very effective for hunting deer, but still can't have the same power or accuracy as a single projectile.

Slugs

Slugs, another type of ammunition used with shotguns, are different from shot in that they are just one, large projectile. They are often used for hunting deer or other larger animals. Traditionally they have been limited to close-range shooting, but in recent decades new designs have produced slugs that supposedly have an effective range of more than 100 yards and are shot from guns that are handled more like a rifle, using a scope instead of a simple open sight. The biggest drawback of slugs is the strong recoil they pack. I've had friends who've shot a 12 gauge slug only once and within hours had a large bruise where the butt of the gun had recoiled against the crotch of their shoulder. For this reason, some people find that practice shooting with slugs is not really viable; the kickback is so fierce and jarring they pass on them altogether. Slugs have an advantage over buckshot, however, in that they won't spray an entire area of an animal with shot, more effectively delivering their impact to one area.

The big advantages of shotguns are fairly significant: when shooting shot or slugs at close range with a simple bead as sight, they don't need to be sighted in and, although one still very much needs to practice to become capable with them, by their very nature they don't require the same kind of precision. With modern slug technology, they can also be used in a similar way to a rifle.

The other main advantage is that in areas that are in close proximity to human habitations, shotguns are often the only legal firearm. Shotguns can also be very versatile. With the right gun, you can use the same firearm to hunt deer with buckshot and ducks with birdshot.

Crossbow

Taking a step away from the deafening roar of rifles and shotguns toward the silence, stealth, prowess (and difficulties/limitations) of archery, we find the crossbow, a hybrid of the two. Combining the ease of aim of a rifle or shotgun with the sleekness of a bow, the crossbow is an effective tool that satisfies many hunters' needs for a weapon that is both efficient and elegant. Becoming confident with a crossbow takes practice and proper sighting, but nowhere near the amount of practice and discipline that shooting a traditional bow takes. For this reason, many would-be bowhunters turn to the crossbow.

The history of the crossbow illuminates this dynamic. Before the crossbow's emergence in medieval Europe, Asia and elsewhere, the bow and arrow was the primary weapon used in warfare. The intensity of training required to produce highly skilled, long-range archers was no small thing. It involved a process of training that was often life-long, beginning in childhood with a rich culture, tradition and esteem surrounding it. Having an active force of skilled archers was a big deal. With the evolution of the crossbow, however, the life-long training and mastery that was previously required was made somewhat obsolete. The crossbow was relatively easy to use, which meant that commoners could now accomplish what before was only possible for an elite class of highly skilled individuals. Modern cross-bows function quite a bit differently than their medieval counter-part, as synthetic materials have allowed them to be more efficient and easier to handle. Being used primarily as a hunting tool now, instead of a weapon of warfare, has also required some modifica-tions in design.

Like all other bows, crossbows are short-range hunting tools. Their maximum effective range is about 50 yards, and most respon-sible hunters won't take a shot at a distance of more than 30 to 40 yards. This is of course a far cry from the range of rifle hunting.

Besides limited range, the main disadvantage of the crossbow, both in the context of historical warfare and for you or me hunt-ing right now, is probably the inability to rapidly reload and shoot successive bolts (*bolts* are the small arrows shot from a crossbow). Where a rifle, shotgun or bow (in talented hands) can be reloaded swiftly for a follow-up shot, crossbows take longer to reload, actu-ally requiring the shooter get out of shooting position to cock their weapon. This is indeed a disadvantage.

Some might also find it difficult to cock a 175-pound crossbow. There are cocking aids available that can make this feat much easier (they are simple devices; nothing more than a rope with hooks on it usually).

Draw weight

The strength of a bow or crossbow is determined mainly by its *draw weight*, that is, how many pounds of pressure are required to draw the string back into shooting position. The particulars of an indi-vidual crossbow's design will determine how efficiently this energy is directed into a projectile, but draw weight is the metric used to measure it overall.

In some regions the minimum draw weight to hunt anything deer-sized or larger is 120 pounds, a strength which most modern hunting crossbows meet or exceed. Draw weights of 175 and 200 pounds are often used in hunting moose, elk and other creatures of such stature.

When hunting small animals, most crossbow hunters use the same weapon they would for larger animals.

Recurve crossbows

The simplest kind of crossbow is a *recurve* crossbow. This style of crossbow has been made for centuries from wood as a combat weapon and hunting tool. The *recurve* in the name refers to the shape of the bow limbs, which have a recurve shape at both ends, bending away from the shooter. As with traditional recurve bows, this design puts more resistance into the limbs and causes them to store more energy, thus shooting a projectile faster and farther.

Compound crossbows

A popular modern variation to the simple recurve crossbow, the *compound* crossbow takes advantage of more advanced technology to store energy in the crossbows limbs more easily. A system of pulleys and cables near the tips of the bow takes the place of a recurve, and through a more efficient distribution of energy allows one to draw the crossbow's string back more easily. Upon shooting, it also reputedly delivers its stored energy to the bolt in a more efficient way, resulting in higher arrow velocity.

The only real disadvantage to compound crossbows is that they have more parts to maintain (or malfunction).

Bows

Bows of various styles and designs have been used continuously as effective, elegant hunting tools for millennia. The earliest, simplest bow was no more complex than a branch of some resilient, tight-grained wood with nocks carved into both ends, which was then bent and strung to efficiently launch arrows. Over time, bow making of course developed into a fine, precise art incorporating many styles and techniques. Still, the basic premise of the bow has remained the same, and the experience of shooting one speaks to this. There is a certain sweetness, satisfaction and requisite discipline/focus in shooting a bow that many feel activates a very simple, primordial feeling.

There are various distinct types of bows to choose from, all with various advantages and disadvantages to offer the prospective bow-hunter. Regardless of the type of bow, these are short-range hunting tools. The effective range will vary with the type of bow and the shooter, but many archers don't take shots at more than 40 yards from their prey, and preferably closer. Some using traditional bows won't take a shot at more than ten to fifteen yards. This is the blessing and the curse of the bow as a hunting tool.

Compound bows

The most technically advanced, modern style of bow, *compound bows* are distinguished from traditional bows in that their limbs are stiff and have swiveling pulleys affixed to the tip at each end. When one draws the string of a compound bow back, these pulleys rotate, distributing the tension in a way that allows the string to relax back into place and be held there with little effort by the shooter. This makes shooting a bow with a 60-pound draw weight considerably easier physically, and allows the shooter to comfortably hold the bow back in shooting position for a great length of time, which allows for a different style of shooting almost more akin to a rifle. Indeed, most compound shooters use a handheld trigger device that clips onto the bowstring, which they then use to draw it back. Once they are ready for the shot, they pull the trigger, making the shooting experience reminiscent of firing a rifle.

With the various tactical advantages they afford, and outfitted with proper sights, compounds are easier to master than more traditional styles of bows. For this reason, they are by far the most commonly used bows today.

Many traditional archery enthusiasts poke fun at compound bows and have a habit of putting up their noses at the hi-tech gadgetry they incorporate. While I don't share this kind of disdain for the compound bow, I will admit that shooting a compound has never given me the kind of deep satisfaction I have felt shooting a wooden bow. They lack the organic flow that makes shooting a traditional bow so enjoyable. Having said that, they're extremely practical and offer many a more comfortable, precise and practical way of bowhunting.

Their main drawback (besides the one I just mentioned) is: you can't make one in your back yard using a couple basic hand tools and a piece of wood you harvested yourself or bought from the lumberyard for ten dollars. You just can't.

Unlike traditional bows, they also have many parts. Parts that can malfunction, break, etc. Still, they are the most popular tool with bowhunters for a reason: they don't require the same dedication and perseverance to become an adept shooter. Although a longbow feels nicer to shoot, when it comes time to hunt and place a shot properly for a clean kill, there are more important things to consider.

Laminate bows

The next most common bow used by modern hunters would be the laminate bow. These bows usually follow a traditional recurve design, with a curve away from the shooter at the tips of the bow's limbs, forcing them to store more energy. Laminate bows are made from layers of wood, fiberglass or other materials that are glued (or laminated) together. They shoot like wooden bows and require a similar amount of practice to master. Like compounds, they can be outfitted with simple sights to aid a shooter's accuracy.

Wooden bows

Sometimes called *self bows*, bows carved from a single piece of wood are of course the oldest and simplest kinds of bow. These can be made from many different woods and in various styles. The traditional *longbow* is the simplest type of self bow. A straight, long and simple design produces powerful, elegant bows.

Wooden recurves are also very popular, and have several advantages over longbows, which all stem from the fact that the recurved limbs store more energy for their length, meaning a recurve can be considerably shorter in length than the straight longbow. Navigating through the woods with a shorter bow can be very helpful for hunting. A bigger bow also means more bulk, and a greater likelihood that one will accidentally brush against a branch or what have you, making noise and sending the prey running.

Beyond the basic distinctions of longbow and recurve, there are countless fascinating alternative styles of wooden bow.

The biggest drawback of wooden bows is, as stated earlier, *they require a lot of practice to shoot with precision!* This is an enormous limitation relative to other hunting tools. After years of making my own wooden bows and practising shooting, I have yet to hunt anything larger than a grouse with a traditional bow. Despite their drawbacks, their appeal is obvious: the grace, sustainability and "fair chase" element that are part and parcel of hunting with a bow.

Other essential equipment

Clothing

Good hunting clothing serves two functions: it allows one to blend in with the environment and it keeps one warm and dry. One's hunting clothing will ideally blend into the environment on more than just a visual level, but will also be quiet when one moves and not carry any strong scent that will reveal one's presence to knowing noses. This will be discussed in more detail later.

Rope

Whether for hanging a creature to skin, tying off its bung or lashing it to an improvised sled to transport it out of the woods, there are many scenarios during a hunt where rope is a godsend. Part of your hunting toolkit should be at least a dozen, and more like 50 to 100, feet of good strong rope. I personally like to carry military-grade parachute cord. It is the diameter of a shoelace, with a tensile strength of 550 pounds. Whatever kind of rope you choose to carry, it should be plenty strong to hang or haul whatever you might be harvesting.

Saw

When hunting animals of deer size and larger, a saw can be very useful for cutting through bone. There are many handy "hunting saws" for sale in sporting stores, but I personally use nothing more than a hacksaw or a simple, all-purpose folding saw. The benefit of using a hacksaw is that when cutting through bone, the teeny tiny teeth don't produce fragments or shards, which are not so nice to get into meat you will be eating; instead they leave a bone powder. Still, an all-purpose, collapsible saw will get the job done, and you can simply brush off or remove any bone fragments it leaves in its wake.

Mesh bags (or not)

Hunters often use breathable, cotton mesh "game bags" during late summer/early fall, when flies are still active and might lay eggs on their kill while it is being transported or hung. I have never used one of these bags, though they look very convenient. A more affordable alternative that is equally effective and more durable/reusable is to find old sheets at a thrift store (or in your closet) that have a weave loose enough to be breathable. Wrap a sheet or two around your kill and hold it in place with some kind of lashing, clothespins or what have you and *voila*—you have an ingenious alternative to what could be considered an overpriced gimmick.

Headlamp/flashlight

Since a lot of hunting occurs during the waning hours of daylight, having some kind of artificial light on hand can be very helpful. Unless you are working under a full moon in the snow, gutting an animal in the dark is not all that fun (in the snow on a full moon it is pure magic). A headlamp is ideal, since one's hands are both left free to work.

Flagging tape/toilet paper

If you wind up having to track your prey after taking a shot at it, having some kind of flagging material to serve as a marker can be very helpful. Bright orange flagging tape works, though you'll have to go back and collect it afterwards. Toilet paper stands out quite well also, and is biodegradable, so you won't have to pick up after yourself. It also serves multiple uses, if you don't like using leaves for wiping.

Daypack

A small pack of some kind where you can store all your tools, snacks, water, binoculars and so on is as essential as the individual items themselves.

5

Techniques

SEVERAL YEARS AGO, I was invited by an acquaintance to go deer hunting. Although I had some reservations about the man who was inviting me, I decided to go. He was much older than me, a seasoned hunter with a long lifetime of experience, so I figured he probably had a lot of knowledge and wisdom I could learn from. The idea was that by coming along I could shoot a deer myself or, if he got one, I would give him a hand with any heavy work and could take the hide, fat and organs and any other parts that he didn't intend to use home with me.

On the day of our hunt, he picked me up at the road near my home early in the morning. We drove in his pickup truck a couple hours, first along the highway and then veering off into a network of logging roads.

The plan was, according to my hunting partner: drive. We would drive until we saw a buck off in a clear-cut or crossing the dirt road in front of us. We both had rifles resting between our legs, at the ready, and when we spotted our quarry, my partner would stop the truck, open his door, aim and shoot if it was on his side. If the deer was on my side, it was my shot. This really was not what I'd had in mind when I signed on to this excursion. Nonetheless, I quietly went along with it, deciding I was there to passively learn from this man.

We drove and drove and drove. My partner chain-smoked the entire time, with the windows rolled up to keep the cold October air out, and delivered an endless stream of raunchy stories.

For hours and hours this was our hunting campaign: driving through one clear-cut after another, stuck in a little box filled with cigarette smoke and one dirty story after another. At some point during this time, I did something that I hadn't done for years: I started praying.

I started praying that we *not* find any deer, that we be entirely prevented from coming across any deer at all. Feeling the effects of all the driving, all the smoke and all the stories, I couldn't think of a more horrific thing than stumbling out of the smoky truck in a daze and shooting a creature in such an awful, stupefied state. I didn't re- ally know who I was praying to, all I knew was that it was very urgent that we *not* find any deer. I had killed many deer before, so it wasn't the act that felt off. It was how we were approaching it; the state we were in did not feel in any way like the state of one who is about to do something so incredibly serious. I knew it would feel absolutely crazy to take a creature's life in the fog I was feeling.

We continued our search until the day's light completely faded without seeing anything. My hunting partner scratched his head, completely dumbfounded at our bad luck, apologizing to me and insisting this was bizarre. I was silently grateful; my prayer had been answered. And I realized, of course, that I was the worst hunting partner ever.

There are a lot of ways to hunt. The strategy, preparation and technique you employ to approach your prey can and do make all the difference in whether or not you are successful. It can also shape the entire experience. The story I just related about truck hunting is about as much space as I will devote to that specific technique, as that is most of the experience I have with it. There is nothing inher- ently bad about any method of hunting, but when you hunt by either patiently waiting for or searching out your prey on foot, you are required to enter, at some level, into the quiet of the land. Your senses are magnified, forced into the here and now. Awareness and wakefulness are demanded. Any method of hunting that compromises this is not really bad news for the prey, so long as it is dispatched quickly, and can sometimes simply be a necessity to get food on the table efficiently, but might in certain circumstances be thought of as unfortunate for the hunter. It is their connection to the experience that is dulled, after all. That's what I was feeling during the story I related above. Of course our technique was a very poor one strategically, too.

What follows is a discussion of various deer hunting strategies and techniques, as well as ideas for pre-hunt preparation. Giving careful consideration to this and planning adequately before heading out can make all the difference regarding the success of the hunt.

Before the Hunt

Where to hunt?

This is perhaps the biggest prerequisite to any hunting. Without a place to hunt, one simply can't. If you live on a piece of land that affords you the opportunity for hunting right there, you are fortunate, but most readers probably won't be in such a situation. If you have the desire and means, you can usually drive into the country and find plenty of land that can legally be hunted on. Another option is to find a landowner who will allow you to hunt on their property. Place an ad online looking for this, or if you are really outgoing, even go politely to people's doors or call farms on the phone and kindly ask. You might get a scornful "*No!*", but that's okay. Many farmers are delighted to have hunters come and remove creatures that they wish would go away altogether. Eventually, asking around and putting it out there will result in finding great places to hunt.

Once you've found a place where you can hunt, you then need to walk the land and determine if it is in fact a viable area for hunting. This is called *scouting*.

Scouting

Scouting an area means getting out there and walking the woods, meadows, clearings or what have you. Only by doing this will you understand where it is you are hunting and develop a sense of what's going on there.

Get to know the lay of the land and the patterns of the prey that live there. Study the tracks and sign. In some instances, looking at a topographic map or other aerial view of an area can provide valuable insight into major landmarks and possible patterns there. The more time you put into scouting, the more conscious and prepared you will be going into hunting.

Stealth

Hunting is largely an act of stealth. It's through reducing one's scent, being conscious of one's movements/stillness, how much noise one makes/doesn't make and so on that one can avoid being noticed by one's prey. There are three basic elements to this: You want to avoid being *seen*, *smelled* or *heard*.

Scent

As mentioned earlier, deer (and many other animals) have an extraordinary sense of smell, which alerts them to danger. Knowing this, hunters can adapt by doing two things: eliminating their scent (or altering it to make it actually attractive to their prey) and playing the wind to ensure it is blowing their scent away from their prey.

Scent elimination

Many hunters consider camouflaging their odor to be essential for successful deer hunting. Putting some effort into this will greatly increase one's ability to enter into a deer's territory unnoticed.

To begin with, keep an outfit of clothing separate from other clothes, reserved specifically for going out into the woods, scent free. Wash this clothing with unscented laundry soap (deer will get spooked by unnatural fragrances) and store it in a sealed plastic bag. Putting some cedar boughs or other aromatic, local plant material in with the clothes can help permeate them with a woodsy odor. Likewise, hanging your hunting clothes over a smoky fire (high up so they don't get scorched) will impregnate them with a smoke scent that effectively covers yours and is quite benign and natural for deer.

For the same reason that one should use scent-free laundry detergent, use scent-free shampoo, soap, deodorant and whatever else you put on your body prior to hunting. Some hunters (myself included) don't even cook with or eat garlic leading up to a hunt, as its odor can seep out of one's pores and alert deer. In many traditional societies, a hunter would also abstain from sex for several days prior to a hunt. This was partially to build a state of clarity and focus, but also because sex is a heavily scented activity.

Deer droppings can also be used as a cover scent. Simply mash them up and rub them onto your clothing and boots. Not for everyone, I know.

Naturally tanned buckskin (usually called brain tan) is possibly the ideal scent-camouflaging clothing. Because buckskin is heavily smoked in the tanning process, it comes with an automatic scent cover. It's also really warm.

Rubber boots are considered by many to be the ideal footwear for hunting, as they shed scent very easily, whereas most other kinds of footwear have laces and other absorbent materials that go about picking up uniquely human scents. Moccasins made from natural buckskin are good for this, too, although the fact that they are not at all waterproof makes them a poor choice for some regions (the cold and rainy Northwest, for instance). Whatever your hunting footwear, try to be conscious of eliminating scent from it before heading out.

Some hunters, of course, don't really do anything to cover their scent and still have success. I had a man tell me once that he had shot many a deer with a lit cigarette dangling in his mouth! If you want to cover all your bases and increase the likelihood of connecting with your prey, however, it's pretty easy and very wise to reduce your odor.

Wind direction

In addition to reducing or eliminating your scent, you can also position yourself so that you are downwind or crosswind from your prey. If there is any breeze, deciphering wind direction is easy. Simply pay attention to which way things are being blown. Wind direction can be fickle and shifty, so make sure you keep on observing for a while to get a sense of where it's consistently blowing, and then keep observing for changes.

When the wind is more subtle, you can test in a few ways. Many hunters use milkweed seedpods for this. I haven't had the pleasure of doing this myself, but the basic method is to gather the ripe seeds in the late summer and store them dry. You then take a handful of the lightweight, feather-like seeds and let them loose into the air. They will ride on the slightest current of wind and flow along, showing you both the wind's direction and if there are any shifts in its current that might make you reconsider your position. You can also tie a fine, lightweight thread to your hunting tool—the end of a rifle or shotgun barrel, or the tip of a bow or crossbow. The thread will act as your automatic wind tester.

Whatever hunting technique you are applying, being mindful of the wind and making sure you are crosswind or downwind from your prey is a good practice.

Using scents as an attractant

While human body odor and artificial fragrances can send deer running away, some smells can actually get deer to run *toward* a hunter. Indeed, there is a profitable industry built upon this, and hunters spend large amounts of money every fall on expensive scents with names like "XXX Doe In Heat" or "Supercharged Buck Rut Fever." As these names suggest, most of the scents used to lure deer are specifically geared to the autumnal rut, when deer are lustily seeking companionship and following their noses to find it.

There are alternatives to the suggestively named store bought scents, however. If one kills a buck or doe, the tarsal glands (located beneath a darkened patch of hair on the inside of the knee) can be removed and used as a lure. Store them in a sealed bag in the fridge or freezer to preserve their moisture and keep them fresh. Scent lures, whether store bought or self made, are used a few ways: One method is to hang your lure in an open canister from a low branch, where it will travel through the breeze attracting curious bucks. Whitetail hunters often apply a buck-urine based scent lure to scrapes (areas of ground that bucks scrape clear and urinate on during mating season), or make "mock scrapes" themselves and perfume them to lure territorial bucks in. These lures can also be applied on the ground wherever one would like to lure a buck in for an ideal shot. Some hunters even apply scent lures to their boots or clothing in hopes of getting really up close and personal. I've heard a couple stories about this tactic being so effective a hunter was mauled or mounted by a lusty buck, though the validity of these reports hasn't been confirmed.

This kind of luring can very effectively bring in bucks. If one would prefer to shoot a doe, however, it usually won't be as useful.

Appearance

Deer have been traditionally thought to be color blind, but recent research has proven this to be only partially true. Deer *do* see a limited spectrum of color, but much less than the human eye. This is why the blaze orange caps or jackets worn by many hunters can go unnoticed; what stands out as a brilliant beacon of light in the dark woods to our eyes easily goes unnoticed by deer, who don't pick up the red/orange spectrum of color well at all. They supposedly do, however, register the blue end of the color spectrum quite well. With this in mind, avoid clothing that is blue or in the blue range of the color spectrum. Generally earth tones are best—or clothes that match the tones of the environment you'll be hunting in.

The old adage around deer hunting and camouflage is that you should break up your form as much as possible. Because deer have

One extreme camouflage tactic is to dress in a deer's fresh skin. Timucua hunting deer in Florida, c. 1562, by Jacques Le Moyne. Courtesy of the Florida photographic collection.

poor depth perception, the two-dimensional appearance of a hunter can easily blend into the landscape if their form is simply obscured in some way. The old-fashioned plaid jacket worn by hunters accomplishes this well, as, of course, does camo gear or an old sweater to which you have attached leaves, moss or other local plant material so that you look more like a bush or a fern-covered rock than another animal. Making your own camouflage outfit in this way can be astonishingly effective, not to mention fun. Traditional buckskin clothing with long, dangling fringes was designed to break up a hunter's form in this way, too.

Wearing clothing that breaks up your form, whether it's camo gear or a plaid jacket and some old-fashioned wool pants, will greatly help you in remaining unnoticed. If you want to go the extra mile, a little mud on the face, hands and any other exposed patches of skin can help too, as they stand out, especially if you have fair skin.

If you prefer to wear blaze orange (or are required to in the area you're hunting), choosing articles of clothing that incorporate some camo element or strips to break up your form can be a good idea.

Once you have an outfit that satisfies this need to obscure your shape and blend in, the other significant feat will be to move stealthily and keep still whenever a deer has you in its field of vision. Remember that deer have an extremely wide range of vision, and take this into account when you are on their periphery.

Movement

Moving silently, slowly and gracefully, in a way that doesn't startle your prey, is an art of its own. The crunch of a dry branch underfoot can be all it takes to send a nearby deer bounding off into the distance. For this reason moving in a slower, intentional and silent way is a skill worth practicing.

The first step to this is easy to say, harder to practice: *slow down*. Move slowly and fluidly, aware of where you are putting your foot down when taking a step, while at the same time paying keen attention to all that is going on around you. Practice this when you are scouting or just walking in the woods, on your way to a hunting spot or, obviously, when you are actually hunting. The more you practice moving silently and fluidly with discipline and awareness, the better you will become at it.

In addition to this slowing down, moving slightly crouched over can also help you both blend into your surroundings (by breaking up your upright form into something less conspicuous) and switch into a mode of careful, conscious movement.

Awareness

In addition to being as stealthy as possible, you also should attempt to use your senses to the fullest extent possible in order to absorb information from the environment during the hunt. Much of this could just be called "Wake up, pay attention and stay awake." There are some specific techniques, however, that can be used to enhance one's awareness—and add fun to the hunt.

Hawk eyes

Usually when we look at things, we do just that: we zone in on specific objects and fixate. Whether we're looking at the words on a page, someone's face, a cloud or a puddle, much of our visual observations are narrow, specific ones. For many predators, finding their prey depends on having a broader type of vision. As a hawk flies above a meadow or sits atop a tree, its eyes drink in the land in wide sweeps. When they detect a movement within the field of vision, they move their focus and attention there to determine what is happening, but that initial state of open looking is a key first step.

Taking a note from the hawk, many hunters and trackers practice something called *hawk eyes*, which is essentially nothing more than the unfocused looking described above. Relax your focus, indeed don't consciously fixate on anything, but instead allow yourself to be aware of your *whole* field of vision. All of the peripheral vision, everything the eyes are catching, can be absorbed in this way. By not focusing on anything specifically, one's awareness is not narrowed. One remains open and receptive.

Try it! Go for a walk in the woods or sit someplace quiet and turn on your hawk eyes, expanding your awareness to encompass your entire field of vision. When hunting try to practice this from time to time, and when something stirs in that broad relaxed field of vision, narrow your focus in on it.

Deer ears

Deer of course have hearing that is far more sensitive and acute than human hearing. This is due to the inner workings of their ear, but also to the big protruding flaps of ear that collect and funnel sound inward very effectively. We don't have ears like that, but we can improvise a makeshift version with nothing more than a cupped hand.

This is called putting on deer ears, and is shockingly effective at increasing one's ability to hear.

By cupping your hands behind your ears, you will notice an instant amplification of the sounds in front of you. By cupping them in the opposite direction, at the front of the ears, you will amplify the sounds behind. Throwing on your deer ears can be very helpful when trying to discern what and where a sound is coming from. Deer ears is a useful trick for all sorts of things, not just hunting! Whenever I think I have heard something in the distance and want to figure out what it is, I put my cupped hands up to gather in the sound.

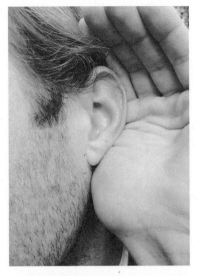

Practices like deer ears and hawk eyes are just two small examples of ways that we can tune into our senses and amplify our awareness of what is going on around us.

You can improve your hearing significantly by cupping a hand around your ears.

In the field

Hunting strategies can be separated into two main categories: *ambush* techniques and *seeking* techniques. In the former, you set up in a stationary position and wait (in ambush) for your prey to come along. In the latter, you are on the move, actively searching out your prey.

Ambush techniques

This method of hunting generally involves concealing oneself along a deer travel route or feeding area and lying in wait. How one chooses to lie in wait can take many forms. The most popular approach nowadays is to wait from a tree stand, a small platform up a tree upon which the hunter sits. Tree stands are popular because they raise one out of the deer's line of sight and can also mean that one's scent is lifted up and away. They can also be built quite easily out of natural material or scrap lumber, though nowadays modern, lightweight metal stands marketed to hunters are more common. One can also situate oneself in a conveniently shaped tree to achieve a similar effect, or perch atop a boulder, slash pile, ridge or other natural feature on the land.

The drawbacks of hunting from way up high in a tree stand are numerous, starting with the fact that tree stands, although they can be moved, aren't really that portable. If you choose a spot on the ground or some natural vantage point to set up on and then decide after hours of waiting that you'd like to try someplace else, you just get up and find a better spot. It's not so easy with a tree stand.

Being high up, tree stands also have an element of danger that hunting on the ground doesn't. One should always use a harness to secure oneself when hunting from a tree stand. Even with this precaution taken, however, crawling up and down the tree can be somewhat precarious.

Another approach is to simply station oneself on the ground in a spot that provides adequate concealment as well as a clear shooting path to the area one is hunting. If one wants to take an extra step in concealment, a blind can be fashioned out of natural materials. Make it simple and make it blend in.

There are many lightweight, prefabricated blinds sold for this purpose, but they could be considered just another expensive and unnecessary gimmick, of which there are truly countless geared toward hunters.

When using this ambush method of hunting, be prepared to do a lot of waiting. When choosing when to arrive at your spot account for some time in which you and the forest can blend, so to speak. Travel to your spot stealthily, and once you arrive stay still and quiet, allowing yourself to really sink into the land. By arriving early and staying still like this, the life around you (birds, squirrels, etc.) will become acclimatized to your presence and not give alarming signals to your prey. Some hunters like to bring a book along to read while waiting.

Choosing your ambush spot

Selecting where you will set up your ambush, whether on the ground, in a stand or in another conducive natural feature of the landscape, takes careful thought. Generally one will want to set up someplace where there is considerable deer traffic or activity; along a well-used travel route or at the edge of a feeding area, for instance. Hunting in the travel zone has some advantages, namely that deer may be slightly less guarded while traveling, which makes them more vulnerable.

"Choke points"

An ideal spot to set up is near a funnel or choke point along a travel route, where deer movement is concentrated. Some examples of this would be: a clear open corridor in an otherwise densely vegetated woodland; the edge of a forest where numerous deer trails converge; or any other natural or man-made feature that causes traffic to consolidate. Edges of forests or clearings often lend themselves to this natural funneling effect.

Staying warm

If the weather is cold, dress warm! When you aren't moving at all for hours on end, things get mighty uncomfortable unless you are thoroughly insulated. If it's raining out, wear clothes that will keep you dry. Don't underestimate the importance of warm clothing: it usually only takes one session of freezing cold or soaking wet hunting to adapt!

Seeking techniques

Seeking techniques involve actively searching out one's prey. Instead of passively lying in wait, the hunter moves about and sees what they can find. At its most basic this means walking the woods or open land until you see your quarry and a good shot presents itself. There are several ways this can be approached.

Still hunting

Still hunting is when a hunter prowls through woods, field edges, marsh lands, etc. looking for their prey. It probably got called *still* hunting because despite the fact that it relies on movement, it equally relies on one's stillness. One will sometimes see a lot more on the move. Still hunting can sometimes require a high level of stealth, discipline and awareness.

When still hunting one should attempt to move in a slow, cautious, quiet way. The still hunter moves step by step, slowly and carefully placing each foot to minimize sound, pausing often to observe. By crouching down periodically you can see from a different angle and possibly catch a glimpse of a deer you wouldn't have noticed otherwise. You can also simply crouch over while walking through the woods to obscure your shape. As you stop to crouch or simply look at your surroundings, you can also listen. The sound of a deer's hooves marching along can usually be heard from some distance.

As the still hunter moves, stops and watches, they look for any kind of movement. Sometimes a deer will show itself with the flick of an ear that is barely visible through dense bushes. That little glimpse can allow you to position yourself, cautiously, for a shot that will lead to your harvest.

Slowly and steadily, the still hunter thoroughly covers an area in order to see a deer before it sees them, and get a good shot. Through preliminary scouting they should of course have found an area that warrants this kind of attention.

While stalking, try to stick to the shadows and edges, using any feature of the land that will help you blend in to your advantage. The slight crunch of a twig or leaf underfoot here and there is in some ways unavoidable when moving through the woods, and not a huge deal. It's by keeping these sounds to a minimum that you can blend in to the sound of the forest and not ring alarm bells that announce your presence to all other denizens of the forest.

Once you have found your prey and are within shooting range, it could still take several minutes to move into a position that is conducive to a shot. It's all about patience.

Especially when your prey is within close range, moving stealth-ily can be a kind of fine art. Although it can be difficult, hunting like this can be very successful and in some situations is the most viable strategy. Patience really is the key ingredient here.

Spot-and-stalk

A variation of this type of hunting which applies to more open areas (clearings, prairies, etc.) is called spot-and-stalk. In spot-and-stalk hunting, one finds a vantage point where one can see an expanse of open land. Binoculars or spotting scopes are often used for this, al-though some choose to rely solely on the naked eye. Once a huntable deer (or other animal) is spotted, the hunter stalks in until they are at a comfortable shooting range. If the deer is already within shooting range, it would be a case of spot-and-shoot hunting.

Again, this can take a good dose of patience. By sticking to just the other side of ridges or using other natural features of the land to remain unseen, staying downwind or crosswind, keeping quiet and generally using every bit of common sense one has, one can carefully make it to within a comfortable shooting range unnoticed.

Try to plan a couple steps ahead. As you move toward your prey, find the next feature of the landscape you are going to hide behind, the next bush you can use for cover after that, planning a strategic route toward your prey as you stalk. This is the mindset of stalking: methodical, sharp, precise. The closer you get to your prey, the more you will want to blend in and be more cautious and precise.

Other factors

Weather

Weather of course has an enormous influence on both how crea-tures behave and how effective one's hunting efforts may or may not be. Many hunters don't even bother going out when the woods are too dry and are littered with a layer of brittle, crackly leaves. When the same forest has been wetted down with fresh rain, one can walk there without making much noise. Walking silently on a thick layer of crunchy dry maple leaves is not really possible.

Some deer hunters prefer to hunt during wet weather. In a good rain one's scent is somewhat covered, as are one's appearance and sound. Such weather essentially acts as a three-way camouflage. So long as you have good waterproof gear, such conditions can be good, although rain does mean poorer tracking conditions, something to consider if you expect to have to do some tracking after your shot.

When it is really stormy, most animal activity will decline significantly. The flip side to that is that when the weather is about to change, that is, when a storm front is moving in, the activity of deer and other creatures increases significantly. Many wise deer hunters swear by hunting these weather fronts, knowing that there will be more deer movement the afternoon and evening before rain comes, and therefore an increased chance of connecting with a deer. Any time during hunting season when this kind of change in weather and precipitation (rain or snow) is on the horizon is a good time to be out on the lookout for deer.

Hunting when there is snow on the ground of course offers superb tracking conditions. During a snowstorm, however, tracks will instantly be smothered and most creatures will be bedded down. There are many ways that the weather can obstruct hunting, and countless ways it can help if one allies one's efforts with it.

The rut

The annual mating season of deer, the *rut*, is the most popular time for hunting them. As mentioned earlier, there are many reasons for this. The deer's preoccupation with mating causes them to become more active during daylight hours and take more risks than usual in general, letting their guard down somewhat. Indeed, deer pretty well forget their normal sense of time as they move about in a ruckus of activity during all hours looking for a mate. You will often see more road-killed deer during this time as they travel about with less inhibition. In addition to the increase in activity, one can also take advantage of the scent lures described earlier, which only work during this period.

Anatomy of the rut

In many northern regions, rut-related activity really gets going around mid-October and climaxes around mid-November/December, when deer actually begin mating and thus don't move in quite the same frenzied fervor. The two weeks before mating commences are the two weeks when bucks are going truly mad with lust, and it is during this period that many deer hunters want to spend as much time as possible in the woods. Where exactly on the calendar this falls will vary from region to region and even slightly from year to year. A combination of getting out in to the woods to observe what is happening and speaking to other seasoned hunters will enable you to figure this timing out.

A month after this first copulation in the cold autumn woods, any does that did not get pregnant will ovulate again. This second ovulation is the last chance for does to get pregnant during the mating season. There will be less estrus in the air this second time around, but activity will still increase. After this second ovulation, deer activity will decrease markedly. Bucks will retreat quietly into their bachelor groups, making amends after all the brawls over women, and does will likewise quietly return to their maternal groups.

Hunting the rut

During the rut one will want to be out hunting as much as possible, as the likelihood of connecting with deer is increased. It really is an incredibly exhilarating time to be out in the woods. The energy of the rut is palpable. However you choose to hunt, the rut is a kind of prime time.

Lures

By using scent lures that you have bought or procured via hunting or salvaging roadkill, you can bring lusty bucks in toward you at this time. I have even heard male hunters swear by their own urine as a lure, simply peeing on a tree trunk near a rub or other indication of buck activity. The testosterone in their urine supposedly brings in aggressive, territorial bucks who are picking up on the hormones but not the human signals in the scent. I have never tried this, since at other times of the year, peeing on your hunting grounds would be a terrible idea, but I believe that it could work. It's possible that the urine of an ovulating (or pre-ovulating) woman could entice bucks during this period, also. Some women hunters out there may want to consciously experiment with this for fun.

Some of the various methods of applying scent lures were discussed earlier in this chapter.

Antler rattling

Another effective technique used to bring bucks in during the rut is *antler rattling*. To accomplish this, simply bring a set of antlers with you into the woods and click, clack and rub them together, simulating the sound of bucks sparring. The antlers can simply be old ones you find in the woods.

To do this most effectively, set up at your hunting spot and begin clicking the antlers gently. Instead of going full bore right away, slowly ease into the rattling. After a minute of gently clicking, stop for a few minutes. Then start again for a minute, a bit louder this time, and stop again. You can also scrape an antler against a tree trunk to simulate that sound. Pause often. By starting gently, making pauses and proceeding in a nuanced way, really simulating what a couple bucks sparring could sound like, you will not startle nearby deer, but rather make them curious to see what's going on. You can also use the pauses to listen and watch for any deer you may lure in.

6

The Shot, and After

Making the kill

Taking a shot at a living creature is a big deal. A poorly placed shot can result in serious suffering for your prey, and should be avoided to the greatest extent possible. You should honor the seriousness of taking a shot by preparing yourself and knowing your limits. Even extremely well-seasoned hunters will sometimes be overwhelmed by what is usually called "buck fever": a surge of emotion that can make taking a steady shot difficult to impossible. There is a fine line between pushing yourself, which is something often necessary in order to accomplish any hunting, and knowing when to back down and wait. Navigating that fine line is a big part of hunting responsibly. To hunt successfully you need to be decisive, need to take the shot, but you also need to know when to pass, when to simply let things be.

Preparing yourself psychologically and emotionally

One of the things I emphasize whenever I am speaking to people about taking a life for food is the incredible importance of having a *clear mind* and *clear energy* before even thinking about trying to go out hunting. If you are filled with conflict, whether it be from the

75

argument you and your partner are having, stress about bills or guilt about that awful thing you just did to someone, leave the gun or bow at home. Go out to the woods and clear your mind. If you are trying to hunt filled with turmoil and conflict, you run an elevated risk of harvesting turmoil and conflict. I speak from experience on this, but the stories are too personal and strange to share here. Suffice it to say that if your life is a mess, sometimes the laws of physics will actually bend in order to make your hunt a disaster. But even on a common sense level, heading into a hunt when you are upset can lead to bad decision-making. You're more likely to forget to click the safety on, to swing your gun or razor-sharp broadhead around carelessly, so on and so forth. Heading into a hunt when you are off center is bad news.

So try to purify yourself.

Purify yourself before the hunt. Enter into it with a clear mind. If your life is a mess, try to practice some housekeeping. Don't come into a hunt with a storm going on inside of you. Traditionally, some indigenous hunters would abstain from sex for some time before a hunt as well as staying alone, away from the village and fasting. Such a practice touches the same principle of purification. By doing those things, they could enter into a state of clarity and focus before heading into the hunt, disconnect from drama. Those specific practices aren't for everybody, but the resultant state of focus and clarity sure is. You might think of them as a metaphor for simply getting clear.

Easing into killing

If you haven't hunted before and want to ease yourself into the raw, carnal reality of it, I suggest starting small. Go fishing, if that's possible, and experience killing a fish. This can be a very good introduction to the reality of taking a life. The next step would be small mammals like rabbits or squirrels. Picking up a roadkill and skinning and butchering it is also an excellent way to become acquainted with the raw, carnal reality of hunting, and will give you confidence in your ability to deal with your harvest.

Once you are acquainted with this reality, you'll feel more comfortable and sane approaching larger animals.

Shot placement

Beyond finding the right place to hunt, deciding on a strategy for hunting there, honing one's aim and putting time in on the ground, one of course needs to have a solid grasp of where to shoot one's prey when an opportunity arises.

Proper shot placement basically means hitting your prey hard in a vital area in a way that creates a wound that will kill it, either from the initial trauma of the shot itself or by bleeding to death. To kill your prey in the most humane way possible, you need to place a shot properly.

Make wise shooting decisions

This can't really be overemphasized. If there is anything questionable about a shot, pass on it. Don't be afraid of passing on a lot of shots. As the saying goes, you can't have what you want unless you are willing to say No to what you don't want. If the safety of other people is ever even remotely going to be compromised or if the shot isn't clear and truly responsible, don't mess with it. This is particularly important to keep in mind when hunting on a small property or near any roads or homes. Know the limitations of your hunting tool, whether it's a compound bow or a rifle, and your own personal limitations as a shooter. Keep things simple for yourself and have integrity when it counts. And when you are about to shoot something, it counts.

Bullets versus arrows and shot placement

Bullets kill an animal by inflicting major trauma, tissue damage and bleeding. They have much more force behind them than arrows, and if shot from an appropriate firearm for the animal being hunted, can effectively penetrate thick bone to get at vital organs. Slugs work in much the same way within their range.

Arrows generally work by cutting or slicing. A razor-sharp modern broadhead or a more traditional arrowhead is effective in slicing through skin, flesh, vital organs and soft bone (ribs) and will cause fatal bleeding or organ collapse, but will not penetrate thick bone or cause the same kind of extensive trauma and damage that bullets do. What this means is that many shots that are fine and effective from a rifle or shotgun are out of the question for a bow or crossbow.

Where to shoot

Before taking a shot at anything, the hunter should have a solid understanding of their prey's anatomy, so they know exactly where to shoot to hit a vital area.

Anatomy

When the hunter looks at their prey, they should have a general sense of the placement of the animal's internal organs. These, after all, are what you will really be aiming at. Always keep in mind that not only are you aiming at internal organs, but that they are three-dimensional targets. When shooting at an angle, always be mindful of this and make sure to compensate for it.

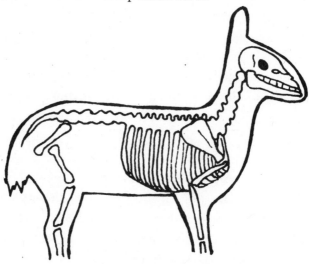

The bone structure of a deer.

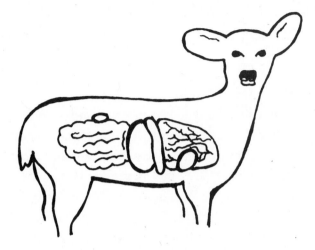

The internal organs of a deer.

The different vital area shots

Heart and lungs (chest)

This is the hunter's ideal kill zone. If an animal is standing broadside, the ideal target is about half way up the body in line with the back of the foreleg. Shooting a bit lower will strike the heart directly. A well-placed lung or heart shot will result in one of the cleanest kills. This vital zone presents by far the largest vital target, providing a larger margin of error than other vital zones. This fact alone makes it the overall best shot placement.

The cons of heart/lung shots include: a lung that is just clipped will sometimes not be lethal, simply wounding a deer. Also, such shots do not always result in an animal dropping dead on the spot. Even with a perfectly placed shot, a common response to a chest shot is that your prey will make a short gallop before laying down and dying, making some tracking necessary. Still, the "boiler room" of the heart/lungs is the choice target for most hunters. For hunters using a bow or crossbow with larger animals, it is the only vital zone an arrow will reliably penetrate.

By aiming slightly forward and upward, one can shoot for the upper shoulder blade, an equally humane shot that will cause your prey to drop on the spot. This shoulder shot is reserved for a powerful firearm up to the task of shattering or penetrating dense bone (it is not a bow shot).

Head/brain

A head shot, in which the skull is penetrated and the brain is struck, will kill any animal almost instantly. The brain is a very small target though, which makes this shot a poor choice under most circumstances. Because of the hard skull that must be penetrated, when hunting animals of any size, this is not a viable shot with a bow; only a high-powered firearm is up to the task of penetrating such bone.

The pros to this shot are that it will drop your prey instantly without any loss of meat. The cons are again that the brain is a small target, and missing it will mean either missing your target entirely (not the worst thing) or, in the worst case, shooting low and breaking its jaw apart. This will result in a slow, painful death of starvation for your wounded prey. The head is also the most animated part of a creature's body, constantly shifting and moving, a fact that alone is enough to keep many hunters away from head shots and consider them ethically questionable.

Neck

A neck shot is another option that, properly executed, will drop your prey instantly. By aiming for the upper vertebrae in the neck, one can sever the spinal cord, break the neck and cause instant paralysis. Here again, however, the vital target it very small, making it a poor shot under most conditions. As with the head, this is a shot that shouldn't be attempted with a bow of any kind, because of the dense bone that must be penetrated.

The pros here again are that if this shot is executed properly, one's prey will drop instantly with little loss of meat. The cons are that this vital area is again so small that shooting slightly off can wound a deer non-fatally. In some instances neck shots will only paralyse your prey, necessitating a follow-up shot. For these reasons, this is another shot that should only be considered by very competent shooters.

Different angles

When deciding to take a shot or not, remember that what you are aiming at is a three-dimensional target that lies inside of your prey. Because of this, the angle of your prey relative to you might render an otherwise great shot totally out of the question.

Broadside

The broadside angle provides an excellent shot for the bowhunter. The heart–lung vital zone is presented in full, which is exactly what the bowhunter is looking for. For a heart shot, aim directly behind the front shoulder and about one third up the body. If you aim a little higher you'll make a double lung shot.

Broadside is likewise an ideal shot when hunting with a firearm. In addition to shooting for the heart-lungs as specified above, you can also shoot through the upper shoulder if you are using an appropriate firearm, creating more shock and severing the spine, which will drop an animal instantly.

Quartering away

This can be a good shot for the bowhunter. The vitals are exposed here without bone protecting them, although in a less open way than broadside, and at an angle that must be compensated for. Remember, your target is a three-dimensional one *inside* the prey's body. To compensate for the angle in this type of shot, your point of aim should be through the  body *to the opposite shoulder*. If your prey is facing away at too steep an angle and your shot might initially pass through the stomach in order to reach the opposite shoulder, wait for a better shot.

This is likewise a good shot when hunting with a gun. As with a bow, *aim through your prey's body to the opposite shoulder*, and if it is facing away at too much of an angle, wait for a better shot.

Quartering toward

This shot is pretty much a pass for the bowhunter. At this angle the heart/lung area is mostly protected by the front shoulder, and picking a spot just behind it will likely result in the vitals being missed and the stomach behind them being struck instead. Best to wait for another shot.

This is a fine shot for gun hunters, presenting numerous targets. One can aim for the head, neck or front of the shoulder.

Head on

This shot is a pass for the bowhunter, as from this angle the vital area is completely protected by bone.

For the gun hunter, however, this is an okay shot that presents a few targets. The head, neck and the center of the chest are all possible targets from this vantage, provided one is shooting a sufficiently powerful firearm/cartridge to penetrate thick bone.

Facing away

No responsible hunter, using either a gun or a bow of any kind, will take this shot.

Waiting for a better shot

Don't be impatient when deciding if a shot is worth taking or not. If your prey isn't aware of your presence and is hanging around the area, give it some time to move around and present a good shot. If it's passing through but not presenting a shot that feels good, wait for another opportunity. Hunting is all about patience, so give in, embrace it and wait. If you don't make room and wait for good shots, they won't show up.

Shooting through dense brush

It is best to avoid shooting through dense brush. It can deflect your bullet or arrow. This effect is greater with arrows, and it is also amplified in the distance between the brush and your target. What this means is that if you are shooting at a deer that has some brush around it, but you yourself and the majority of the shot's path is in the clear, the shot may be barely affected. If you yourself are shooting directly through a patch of thick vegetation, however, the deflection may greatly alter your shot's trajectory by the time it reaches its target. Keep this in mind when choosing whether or not to take a shot in dense brush.

A deer that's on the move

One should avoid taking shots at moving deer. A walking deer can often be stopped or stalled, however, simply by making a grunt sound, or even talking to it. For instance, a casual "Hey" or a kind "Stop" will in many cases cause a deer to pause momentarily, giving you a chance to shoot. Try and not be too alarming, but get heard and give your prey a reason to take pause and decipher what it just heard.

The follow-up shot

Every effort should be taken to make your initial shot as precise and well placed as possible. However, as soon as you get off a first shot you will want to rapidly reload if possible and, if an opportunity is presented, get off a well-placed follow-up shot. In some cases this will make the difference between bringing down your prey or not. In others it will not be called for.

If you are hunting with a gun, you should practice rapidly getting off follow-up shots when target shooting. With bows, the same applies—make it a part of your archery practice to develop a technique of quick reload and follow-up shooting. Crossbows are ill suited to fast reloading, so make your first shot count.

Try not to relax and admire your shot after taking it. Instead stay sharp and reload, ready to strike again if the opportunity arises, because it can take a creature a moment to respond, or it may pause for an instant as it retreats.

After the shot

Once you have taken your shot, unless your prey drops in its tracks, the real work begins. In many cases, especially if you are hunting with a bow or crossbow and are hunting a larger animal, there will be some tracking required after the shot. If you drop your prey on the spot no tracking will be necessary, but even a perfectly placed heart or double lung shot can still require tracking.

Waiting

If your prey flees after you take your shot, the last thing you want to do is pursue it right away. When a creature senses it is being chased, its adrenals will kick in and it will go into serious flight mode, heading as far away as possible. If you sit back and wait, however, your prey will feel more secure in settling down nearby, where, if it has been shot well, it will lose strength and blood until it dies.

So wait. A half hour is the general rule of thumb. Just stay put right where you took your shot for thirty minutes, keeping the exact spot your prey was standing in when you shot it emblazoned in your mind. Try also to clearly remember where it ran and where it left your view. This will all be very helpful when that thirty minutes is over and you get up to track your prey.

Tracking

After thirty minutes have passed, it is time to go and investigate the spot where your prey was standing when you shot it. Look for any sign that was left by the shot. Blood and hair are the main clues to search for here. Once you find any blood or hair on the ground or vegetation around the shot site, you've determined that you made a hit and you've got a start.

The color of this blood will give an indication of where your prey was hit:

- Frothy, pinkish blood indicates a lung shot.
- Rich red blood without a frothy quality indicates bleeding from a major vein or artery.
- Dark blood mixed with what appears to be stomach contents indicates a stomach shot. A stomach shot will usually be fatal eventually, but one should wait four to five hours before beginning tracking. If dark blood is mixed with intestinal contents, indicating a gut shot, wait ten hours before commencing your search.

Following the blood trail one's prey has left is one of the main tactics used in tracking it down after the shot. This can sometimes require a good deal of patience and discipline. Follow any spatter of blood you see. If you come to a spot where this trail appears to end, mark it. A piece of toilet paper or bright flagging tape are ideal, as they stand out as a beacon. Toilet paper has the advantage of decomposing quickly, so it can be left where you place it in good conscience.

With the last splatter of blood marked, go forth methodically, investigating a swath in one direction, then another, then another, until you find the next blood sign. Being methodical in your search is key, otherwise you will waste energy and be less likely to follow a sparse trail successfully. If the blood trail is heavy and easy to follow, this might not be necessary at all, but always be prepared to do some real detective work.

The amount of blood on the ground where your prey was shot doesn't necessarily tell you how well the shot was placed or whether or not it was fatal. An animal can bleed very little on the outside and still die from internal bleeding, so an absence of blood isn't a clear indication that you missed. A chunk of tissue will sometimes move to block up a wound, causing the blood trail to lighten or trail off.

If you can't find any blood, look for other forms of sign. Tracks, overturned leaves, disturbed vegetation and disturbed ground are the clearest sign in some circumstances. The tracks left by a running deer look quite different from the tracks it leaves during a casual wander. They will often look more like hoof-sized disturbances made roughly into the ground than clean, gently pressed tracks. This can be helpful, as the increased force means heavier footprints which might register on ground where they normally wouldn't.

Also, don't just look on the ground. Search vegetation, fallen logs, branches and tree trunks for blood, and *be open to unconventional signs*. I once heard a hunter describe a scenario in which he tracked down a deer he had shot in late summer by listening for flies! He had lost the blood trail and was having no luck in his search for sign when it dawned on him that the faint buzzing he was hearing might be worth checking out. He faithfully followed his ears and, to his relief, found a cloud of flies buzzing around the deer he had shot!

It should be stressed that you really should follow up every shot you take thoroughly, with the attention to detail described here. Even if there is just the faintest spatter of blood, a few hairs, or no sign other than some vague tracks, carefully follow it. Mark where you lose the trail, find the next sign and carry on like this. Even if you don't see any sign initially at the shot site, look harder, exhausting the area for any indication of a hit. If there is no blood or hair, look for disturbed ground and vegetation. Follow whatever sign there is and be incredibly thorough; it is unethical to do anything less.

A few other tracking considerations worth noting are:

- Wounded animals will sometimes run toward water.
- Keep in mind that your prey might make sudden changes in direction; try not to let this catch you off guard.
- Two people can track together quite well. One person can work the blood trail while the other circles the area watching for any sign of a sudden change in direction.
- If a rain- or snowstorm is fast approaching, you may need to start tracking more promptly than normal, as the looming weather will likely wash away or cover the very sign you are counting on.
- While tracking after a shot, be aware that you might find your prey wounded, still alive. With this in mind, move slowly and stealthily so as to not spook it, and be prepared to dispatch it if necessary.

Of course, the more work you have put into practising your shot, knowing your own limitations as a shooter and staying within them, the more likely you will be on target and any necessary tracking will be a short affair. This is the goal, but things do go wrong sometimes, so be prepared.

Is it dead?

Whether the animal you shot dropped where you struck it, bolted 30 yards into the bush and collapsed, made it a couple hundred yards from where you hit it before collapsing or any other possible scenario, when you come upon it, you will want to approach it carefully and make doubly sure it is dead before assuming this is the case. Have your gun or bow at the ready in case you need to dispatch the animal. First stand back at a safe distance and observe for any sign of life. If there is such sign, but you have the sense that it is part of the creature's final moment and that it is passing away already, you might want to just give it some space to die peacefully. If you took the shot an hour earlier, however, the animal is probably agonizing and you should end its pain.

If there is no movement, look for more signs that it is dead. A dead deer will often have its tongue sagging out of its mouth and its eyes wide open. When all indications are that an animal is dead, you can make double sure by finding a long stick and, from a safe distance (well clear of any antlers or hooves), prod and poke. Sensitive spots like the belly, mouth or eyeball are good for this. Getting up close to an alive and wounded wild animal can be very dangerous and even potentially fatal, so do be cautious and thorough with this.

7

Field Dressing

GUTTING A CREATURE CAREFULLY and cleanly is so satisfying it is well worth any extra energy it might take to do well. If you plan to eat the organs of your prey, this is an additional incentive to put some extra intention into the process of field dressing (the common term for removing the entrails/organs from the abdominal and chest cavities). Even if you don't have a taste for deer liver or elk suet, rest assured that there are *many* people who would be ecstatic if you offered such precious foods to them. If you save these organs and put the word out, these people will come lustily for them. Better yet, try adding them to ground meat, sausage or other dishes. They're way too nutritious to overlook.

The process of field dressing is really very simple. With just a little bit of knowledge and technique, it can be quite graceful. It gives one a window into anatomy and physiology which most people who aren't surgeons rarely experience so intimately. It also comes to most people very naturally. I personally have had the experience and have heard countless others say that gutting and skinning creatures felt like learning something they *already* knew how to do; as though our ancestors have done it for so long that it is built into our cellular memory. Once one begins, it feels very familiar.

What follows are instructions for field dressing a deer. The mechanics of the process vary little from squirrel to moose, it's just the scale that changes. A squirrel, for instance, might take an experienced hunter from one to five minutes to clean fully; it can take that long just to make your initial cuts on a deer, though.

Bleeding (or not)

Before getting to the process of field dressing, I should comment on the commonly held belief that one must *bleed* a creature before anything else to avoid spoilage. Typically it is thought that this should be done by slitting the throat soon after death so that blood can escape and not remain/stagnate in the body. The short version of my response to this is: don't bother with this practice, it has no benefit and is a waste of your time.

When you hunt a creature, you typically kill it by inflicting a wound that bleeds considerably in the final moments of the creature's life. Once the animal's heart has stopped beating, there is no longer any pressure generated to force blood out of a wound (or through the body). Slitting a completely dead animal's throat will produce little more than a small trickle of blood, which will have pretty well no effect on draining any residual blood from the body. This is not really a bad thing, because as it turns out, blood doesn't actually spoil meat or give it any off flavor. Indeed, there is always some amount of blood latent in muscle meat, which makes it all the more delicious. So, to reiterate, don't worry about bothering to try to somehow *bleed* your kill (which may have already bled to death).

Field dressing deer

Once you have established your prey is indeed dead, you might want to give a bit of time for it to fully *settle*. This might be just a few minutes, maybe longer, maybe shorter. You'll know when it feels right to begin.

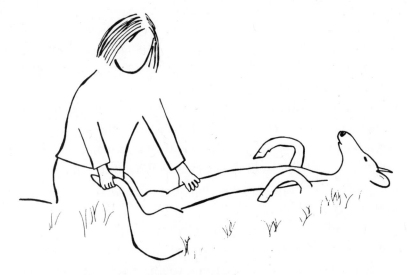

Deer being propped up.

Start by propping the deer's body so that it is lying on its back, belly up and fully exposed for working on. You may place branches, logs or rocks on either side of the rump or head to help hold it in place, or tie a leg (or a couple legs) to a tree with rope to hold it stable.

Freeing the anus

It may seem counterintuitive, but usually one begins the process of field dressing at the dirtiest spot on the kill: the bum hole. By

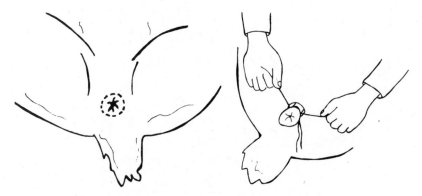

Freeing the anus and tying it off.

cutting the muscles around the anus and attached length of colon (also known as *freeing* the anus), one can tie it closed, ensuring no feces will escape from the colon during later steps in the process of gutting, which could contaminate meat.

Doing a careful, thorough job of cutting the muscle and tissue connecting the colon to the cavity it runs through, sandwiched between the pelvic bone on one side and the sacrum on the other, will completely detach it from the body and allow it to slide out freely along with all of the other guts when they are pulled out. Doing this right is very satisfying.

Take care to cut *around*, not *into*, the colon. Once it has been freed, pull it out of its cavity enough so that you can tie it closed with a piece of string or cord. If you think you have gotten some feces on your hands and/or knife, wash them off with some water, your own urine (which is actually a great natural hand wash, often exalted for its disinfectant properties), crushed cedar boughs or whatever else you have before continuing.

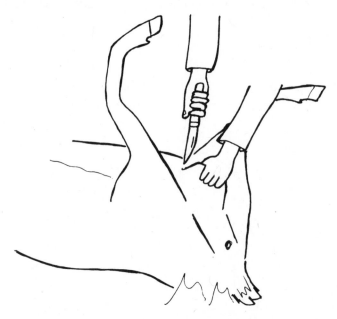

Pulling up the paunch and making the first cut.

Opening the body

To remove the entrails, first make a slit along the belly from the pelvis up to the breastbone or, in many cases, through the breastbone and all the way up to the base of neck. Making this incision without puncturing the stomach or intestines is the key, and worth any extra care or attention it might require.

To begin, use your fingers to pull a section of the paunch up and away from the body. With this skin pulled up, you can begin your incision by cutting into the paunch with a knife with no risk of cutting into any digestive organs.

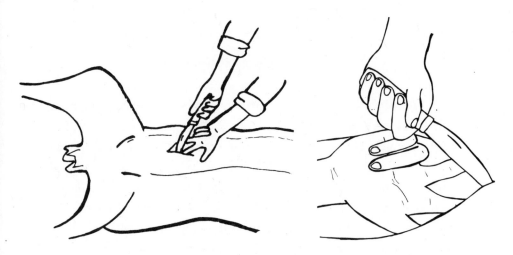

Making this cut safely.

Once you have made an opening, use the fingers of your free hand to get in and enlarge it. Holding your knife at a careful angle so that it doesn't protrude down into the guts, begin making a slit up toward the chest, using your free hand as a lever inside the cut and pulling the skin and underling membrane upward, away from the guts. This will create a gap between the knife blade and the guts below, preventing them from being cut. Go as slow as you need to, keeping your knife blade pointed up and away from the guts beneath it.

Cutting up through the breastbone.

When you get to the breastbone, you have two options: cut through it for easy access to the organs beneath, or stop there, fold up your sleeves and reach up into the chest cavity to get at them. I usually like to cut up through this bone, which can often be done with nothing more than a knife, brute force and a bit of finesse. There is a sweet spot to either side of the breastbone, where the ribs join with it, that you can plow through with your pocketknife all the way up to the base of the neck. Alternatively one can use a hacksaw or any other suitable saw (a hacksaw has the advantage of not producing any little sharp bone shards that can get into the meat).

Once you've finished your upward cut, go back down to where you began it and carefully extend the slit right down to the pelvic bone, cutting around the genitals so they can be removed with the rest of the organs.

Now you can remove the organs. Begin at the top end of the carcass by cutting the windpipe and esophagus. To prevent any digestive juices from the esophagus from leaking out and getting onto the meat, one can tie it off with string in two spots spaced a couple inches apart, then make the cut between the ties.

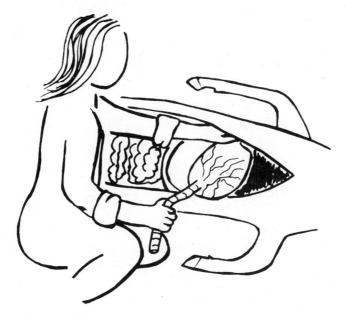

Pulling out the windpipe, which will bring with it the lungs, heart and, once you break the diaphragm, the rest of the internal organs.

After cutting the windpipe and esophagus, pull them down, out and away from the body. All of the internal organs are connected in a kind of linked network to the windpipe, so it acts as an excellent lever to begin pulling the whole mass out with.

Use your hands to help loosen and free the organs where they are connected to the cavity wall. Along the back and around the diaphragm you will have to pull, pry and tear through connecting tissue to get the organs free. If you need to resort to using a knife to help this along, do so very carefully.

The diaphragm itself is a thin muscle that acts as a barrier between the lungs and heart in the chest cavity and the liver, stomach and other organs that lie in the abdominal cavity below.

As you work down, carefully remove the organs you want to save (beginning with the heart and lungs and moving on from there) and put them aside.

Once you have gotten past the diaphragm, the stomach, intestines and all the smaller organs should come out relatively easily. There will be some tissue connecting them along the backbone; carefully and forcefully pull them free from this.

If the bladder is full (it will be unmistakable), avoid puncturing it for obvious reasons. You can often actually empty the bladder by squeezing it and holding the detached genitals away from the body. If you want to use this urine as a scent lure/cover, save it. In any case, keep that pee off the meat. If you do get some on the meat, however, don't get too worried. Just wipe it off and either rinse that area or slice the pee-covered exterior off.

Now, if you freed the anus completely as described earlier, the whole mass of guts should be able to come out of the body freely when you get to the pelvis. If the colon is still somehow attached, make whatever cuts are necessary to detach it. When the guts are all out, you're done!

An alternative method: breaking the pelvic bone

There is one major variation to this method that I must add, as I often employ it myself and on some creatures it is more practical.

There is an alternative to *freeing the anus* in the way I described earlier. Rather than carefully cutting around the colon so that it can freely slip through the pelvic cavity, one simply breaks through the pelvic bone so that the colon is revealed and can be worked on and removed more directly. This is usually done with an ax or a saw. On larger animals like moose this makes more sense, and on smaller animals like rabbits or squirrels it can be done just by using one's knife blade to pry up and break the pelvic bone.

To use this method, skip the whole freeing the anus step at the beginning of gutting and do everything else. Once you get to the point where all the entrails are free and hanging out the side of the carcass, ready to go but still attached to the colon, it's time to break open the pelvic bone.

Using a saw, carefully make your strokes against the center of the pelvic bone, parallel to it and the back of the creature, making sure that you don't cut into any intestine. When you've just gotten through, stop cutting and use your hands to spread the legs/pelvis open. If you use an axe, simply hold the blade in the same spot and use something at hand as a mallet to break through the bone.

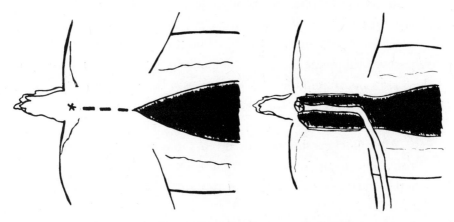

Sawing/breaking through the pelvis. Carefully saw through the center of the pelvis, or use an ax head to carefully split it along the dotted line.

Once you have opened up the pelvic cavity, use your knife to cut around the colon, detaching it completely from the body and then removing it, along with all the other guts. Be careful to not get any feces on the carcass while doing this.

After you have completely removed the guts, you may want to flip your prey's body onto its stomach so that blood can drain out of the open, empty cavity. I usually do this for a minute or two.

Smaller creatures

For smaller animals, everything above applies, it is just scaled down. The main difference is that one need not free the anus of very small creatures (squirrels, rabbits and the like). Their bum holes are so small that it would actually be a great feat to try and cut them free.

Instead one simply breaks the pelvic bone, as with larger animals. One can, however, use a knife tip to pry beneath and then break the pelvic bone. No sawing is necessary. Once this bone is broken, the colon can be easily removed with the rest of the guts.

Birds

Birds should be plucked prior to gutting. Sometimes this can be done immediately after the bird is killed and is still warm. If the feathers do not come out easily without removing chunks of skin, however, submerge the carcass in hot water for about thirty seconds.

How hot should the water be, you ask? Bring a large pot of water to a boil, then remove from heat. This not boiling but still super-hot water is ideal.

After plucking, the entrails are easy to remove. Make an incision from the anus up to the ribs. Then reach in and up into the ribcage to pull the guts out, cutting away the anus where it is attached to the colon if necessary.

Skinning birds is not recommended, as it removes the nutritious and delicious fat.

8

Skinning

MANY HUNTERS take no more care skinning an animal than they would peeling a potato, slicing the hide into chunks and throwing it away. I got to see this firsthand some years ago when I put ads up asking hunters in my area for their unwanted deer hides. I ended up getting about a dozen deerskins that fall, which I was very grateful for, but in the end I didn't tan a single one of them, and never bothered asking strangers for their hides again. Every skin I received was so badly sliced up that I felt embarrassed for the hunter who thought I could use it for anything other than a strange, disposable Halloween costume. Seeing the state of these skins made me realize that since most modern hunters have never done anything with the skin of their kill, they have never learned how to remove it carefully in one whole piece.

The skin of many animals can be an incredibly valuable part of the harvest, one that can outlast the edible portion by years or even decades if it is well prepared. As such, it is well worth taking a few simple steps while skinning to make sure the hide is removed in the most intact, efficient way. Following these steps also makes skinning easier and faster, and will dramatically reduce the amount of meat that ends up coming off with the hide, thus eliminating a common waste of food.

The main distinction between what I call the *standard* method of skinning and the *smarter* method of skinning is that in the smarter method, you don't cut the hide off, you pull it off. This method actually follows the body's natural structures, and as such is incredibly simple and straightforward.

The directions that follow are for deer, but apply to most any other herbivore.

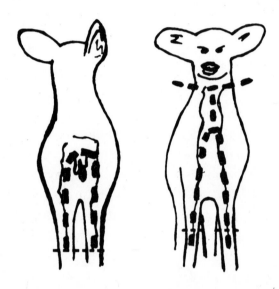

The ideal placement of skinning cuts: along the front of the
front legs and along the back of the back legs. This gives
the most useable-shaped hide.

Making your initial cuts

The first step in skinning is making a series of cuts in the hide which allow one to peel it off and disrobe the kill. Where these cuts are placed will determine the shape of the skin once it is removed. By following the pattern illustrated here (making cuts around the neck and knee joints, along the front of the front legs and the back of the back legs), one ends up with a much more useable, rectangular-shaped skin. Placing these cuts on the inside of the legs, a common practice, gives a much more irregularly shaped hide: still useable, just not quite as ideal.

An easy way to remember this tip is: *cut along the front of the front legs and along the back of the back legs.* It's a little thing, but it makes a big difference.

Hanging

Skinning a creature on the ground is almost always tedious and difficult. You need to be mindful of not getting any leaves, dirt, twigs or debris on the exposed flesh and it's awkward work, done bent over, rolling the carcass around as you work. Hanging the carcass removes these obstacles, allowing you to work around the whole body, keep things clean and have the benefit of using your body weight as you pull the skin down and off of the carcass. If you have rope and are around trees or other similar structures, I strongly recommend hanging any creature for skinning. In the event that you don't have rope, are in a hurry or are alone and can't lift your kill up to hang it, adapt to working on the ground.

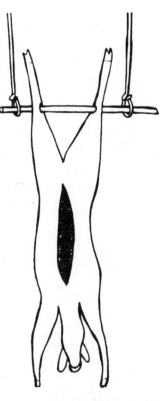

Deer hanging from its lower legs.

You can hang the creature from its neck, so that its body is upright, or from its hind legs, so it is suspended upside down. The latter method has the advantage of securing the body from two points, which stops it from spinning, swivelling or rotating as you work.

The easiest way to hang a creature from the hind legs is by inserting a sturdy branch or pole about two inches in diameter be-

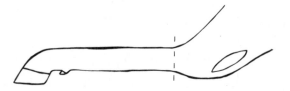

Where to cut behind the tendon on rear legs to insert pole for hanging. Dotted line marks where to slice through skin and break lower leg off at the knee joint.

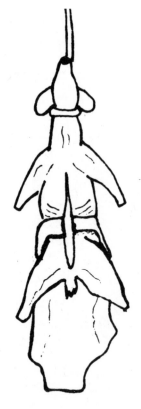

Having your kill hanging will make it easier to peel, pry and pull off the skin; resist the temptation to use a knife and potentially slice it up.

hind the strong tendon that runs along the back side of the leg. This pole can then be hoisted up into position and held in place with strong rope.

Pulling the skin off

With the deer hung, you can now get to work pulling the skin off. I should emphasize the word *pulling* at this point. You can actually put your knife away now, perhaps even put it out of sight so you won't be tempted to use it. You shouldn't need it at all for the rest of the job, and using it will put the skin at risk of being accidentally slashed and damaged.

Using your fingers, begin peeling back the hide at your skinning cuts. Once you have peeled enough back, you can use your fingers and hands to push in and underneath the skin, prying it away from the body. You can use your fists to pry in this way, too. As you work along, peeling, prying and fisting the skin off, be mindful of any meat that wants to come off with the skin. By using your hands to guide where and how the skin is peeling off, you can navigate around any muscles that want to come along for the ride, keeping the hide clean and leaving the meat where it belongs.

Once you have gotten a good start and are past the legs, you will be able to easily pull the skin down the torso. Use your body weight to really yank on it. Take a little care, again, to keep the meat on the carcass. Before you know it you'll be done!

When you can't pull it

There are some creatures whose skin will not pull off. Mostly these are omnivores like raccoons, pigs, bears and such. When you come across one of these creatures, you will have to ignore my advice about pulling off skins and use your knife to carefully cut the skin off. Do this slowly and cautiously, keeping in mind where the skin is and still pulling it away from the body as much as you can while you work, to reduce the amount of force you'll need to apply with your blade. Again, by keeping the skin free from holes you will have a much nicer hide to work with.

"Case skinning"

A style of skinning animals, called "case skinning," is well worth mentioning here. Case skinning is typically reserved for smaller animals, and is the main way that fur-trappers skin their catches. What

Case skinning a rabbit.

distinguishes it is that one just makes an initial slit that allows the skin to be peeled off like a sock, in a tube-like shape rather than a flat sheet as described above. If the face is left intact with the skin, it actually forms a natural case.

To case skin an animal, you gut after skinning. Otherwise the slit you make up the belly will completely thwart the entire plan.

Storing hides

Once you have removed your beautiful, well-shaped, unsliced hide, you will need to either begin working with it relatively soon or preserve it for later. There are a few options here:

Freezing

The easiest thing one can do with a hide is put it in a plastic bag and freeze it. To do this, fold or roll your hide up flesh side in, place in a plastic bag and store in your freezer indefinitely. If you flesh your hide before freezing it (a process described shortly) it will end up being considerably less bulky in your freezer.

Salting

This method, also called *wet salting*, exploits the amazing sterilizing properties of salt to keep a wet, folded hide perfectly preserved for a great length of time. To salt a hide, simply lay it out on the ground, flesh side facing up, and spread a layer of fine salt over it, right out to the very edges. Now fold the hide in half lengthwise, the way it would have been draped over the creature it came from, making the edges as flush as you can. Then fold or roll it up so it is compact and store in a sealed plastic or wooden container (the salt will make metal rust). Five-gallon buckets work well for this.

Any amount of air flow will cause the salted hide to dry out, so be sure to keep a tight lid on the container.

After the salted hide has sat for a day or so in its container, a pool of salty water will usually have accumulated. Pour this off. Hides can be stored in this way for up to one year.

When you're ready to use the skin, brush the salt off and rinse it very thoroughly (either in moving water or in a bucket, changing the water several times over a couple days).

Drying

Drying is the most environmentally friendly method of preserving a skin, but takes a bit more initial work than the other techniques listed here. That said, you will have to do this additional work—which simply involves removing any fat or flesh that is attached to the skin—with any skin before it can be further processed and made into anything.

Fleshing

To quickly and easily remove the flesh from a hide, you'll want to invest in a couple simple tools: the scraping beam and a scraper. You'll need these for any natural tanning process, as well.

Scraping beam. This hide has been pinned on the beam with its hair side up. To remove the flesh, simply place your skin flesh side up and push and scrape downward with a flat scraper.

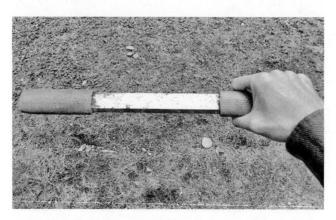

A simple scraping tool. This is made from a recycled mill planer blade, but any piece of metal, hard plastic, bone, etc. with similar dimensions and a good edge that isn't too sharp, but will catch flesh, will work.

A scraping beam is really nothing more than a smooth, round pole, around six feet long and one foot in diameter. This beam is rested against a tree (in a spot where it fits *just* right) at an angle, and the hide is draped over it and pinned into place by the pressure of the beam resting on it. Any log you use for this purpose should be very straight, smooth (free from bumps and burls), hard (not rotting) and bark free. Harder woods are ideal, but any will work. I have also used wide PVC pipe, which has the advantage of being extremely light and durable.

A scraper is also a very simple tool: a thin, flat piece of hard material (usually metal, though bone, stone and hardwoods can also be used) with a good edge. Not a sharp edge: in fact, an edge with a 90-degree angle can work beautifully for scraping hides; since it isn't sharp, you can actually put some force into your work without any danger of damaging the skin. The scraper pictured is a used mill planer blade that has been hafted and could be considered the ideal scraping tool. In a pinch, I have improvised serviceable scrapers from large bread knives (adding a second handle by wrapping the top of the blade thickly with duct tape and using the back, blunt edge for scraping), machetes and many other random flat metal objects with solid 90-degree angles.

To flesh a skin, drape it flesh side up over your fleshing beam. Use your scraper like a plow, forcefully digging in beneath any areas of meat or fat attached to the hide and pushing them off, like a snowplow clearing a street. As you clear an area, shift the hide around, pinning it firmly into place, and continue until all the noticeable flesh and fat have been removed.

Letting it dry

Once your hide has been fleshed, it is ready to dry out. This can be as simple as hanging the skin, flesh side up, over a barn rafter, a sunny railing or your clothesline, in the garage or any other dry, well-ventilated space where it will dry out without being hijacked by a dog or other hungry creature. Make sure the skin is not folded in against itself anywhere when hanging it to dry. It should take anywhere from one to three days to dry out—any longer and your hide needs to be someplace airier or warmer or it will begin to rot. Once dried, you should of course store your skin somewhere dry, protected from hungry dogs and the like. If you hang it above a smoky fire and get it just ever so slightly smoked, it will last dried for years. Without any touch of smoke, a dried hide will last more like six months. This is because over time it will attract little insects whose favorite food is hide. These little fellas will eventually chew holes right through the skin—but they hate the taste of smoke.

Feathers

Birds should be plucked, not skinned. See the previous chapter for instructions on this process.

9

Butchering

IT IS A COMMON PRACTICE for many modern hunters to take their kill to a professional butcher who will hang it in a walk-in cooler for ageing, then process it into various cuts, ground meat, stew meat, sausage and pepperoni. This is unfortunate, for several reasons. First, the hunter's kill will sometimes actually be mixed up with the meat of *other* animals, which really does rob the whole experience of its intimacy. Some hunters actually request this, getting their ground venison cut half and half with pork. If this is what you like, so be it, but I would strongly urge every hunter to cultivate a taste for unadulterated wild meat: *it's just so good.* Taking your kill to the butcher is also an unnecessary expense and will never result in as thorough a job as you can do yourself. But the most unfortunate aspect by far of taking your kill to a professional butcher is that you miss out on one of the most beautiful and enjoyable parts of the hunt. There is nothing daunting or complicated about butchering your own kill. It is something every hunter should take on to have a complete experience of transforming their prey into food. There are no special tools or training necessary, just a few simple concepts and techniques that are easily learned and applied.

Ageing

Ageing meat is the ancient practice of allowing it to hang in a cool, well-ventilated space, protected from insects and animals for a period of time so that naturally occurring enzymes in the meat can begin a process of cellular breakdown or *pre-digestion* that makes the meat more digestible and tender and concentrates and enhances its flavor. All quality cuts of commercial beef will advertise how long they have been aged for (often 21 days or more). I have heard many people say that unless meat has been aged it isn't worth eating, and while I personally wouldn't go that far, there is a reason for such statements. The complex, subtle flavors that evolve in a cut of well-aged meat can be quite outstanding. You could think of fresh meat versus well-aged meat as being parallel to raw cabbage versus sauerkraut, or fresh milk versus a cave-aged Gruyère cheese. The latter in all cases have more flavor, more culture and are nutritionally enhanced.

Nowadays meat is often aged in walk-in coolers, where the temperature is controlled and results are highly predictable. Most hunters of course do not have access to walk-in coolers, but that's okay: for 99.9 percent of human existence, our hunting ancestors didn't have access to them either.

Ageing versus rotting

In order to properly age meat, there are a few considerations to be kept in mind:

- *Ventilation:* If meat is wrapped up in plastic bags or otherwise kept in an unbreatheable environment, pathogenic anaerobic bacteria will blossom, which are not what we want and can actually make us sick. This is why meat is often, though not always, hung in the open air to be aged and is always kept dry. If meat has water on it and stays soaking wet (e.g., is stored in a creek or in the rain), the same kind of bad bacteria will take over. Make sure your meat is kept dry for ageing.

- *Temperature:* The ambient temperature will affect the speed of the ageing process. The enzymatic activity will be greater at a higher temperature and slower at a lower temperature. This means that attaining the same level of tenderness and improved flavor/digestibility might take 21 days of hanging at an average temperature of 37 degrees Fahrenheit and only four days at 54 degrees Fahrenheit. Many hunters will wait until late fall to do their deer hunting for this reason; the lower temperatures allow one to hang meat for a week in an unheated garage at a predictable, cool temperature.
- *Protection:* You will want to hang your meat to age someplace where animals won't bother it, and if it is warm, protected from flies and other insects. An unheated garage, shed, barn or cold room suffice for the former, and mosquito netting or reusable cheesecloth "game bags" suffice for the latter.

Where to age it

Some great places to hang a carcass to age have already been mentioned: unheated garages, basements, sheds, storage rooms, barns and the like. I often hang whole deer on my covered porch, out of the reach of my cats, because I have an unspoken agreement with all the local racoons and bears that keeps them from coming around. If you lack these kind of spaces, however, there are alternative options.

In the fridge

You can substitute your fridge for the walk-in cooler modern butchers use. Simply empty out the produce drawers or shelves and place whole sections of meat on or in them. Allow air space around all the cuts you place in your fridge, to keep the good bacteria in charge. Meat is usually aged in this environment for two to five days. The lack of good ventilation doesn't promote an extended ageing, but is absolutely sufficient to get the job done. The bottom side of the meat where it has been resting against the fridge drawer or shelf will develop a scum or slime which you can scrape or trim off with a knife.

In a cooler

A large cooler can also be used to age meat if space is at a premium. Fill several two-gallon plastic jugs with water and freeze. Place the frozen jugs into the cooler, as your ice cubes, and put meat on top or around them. Change bottles for fresh frozen ones as they thaw out. This is functionally the same as ageing meat in a fridge.

To skin or not to skin?

Deer and various other creatures can often be aged with their skin left on. There are a couple advantages to this: during ageing, skinned meat will typically form a thin, hard rind on all exterior surfaces, along with, depending on how long it hangs, a thin film of slime or scum than usually has to be scraped off. Leaving the skin on your ageing meat prevents either of these things from happening, as the skin acts as a natural, protective wrapper of sorts, and unlike an artificial wrapper (e.g., plastic) does not foster pathogenic bacteria. For these reasons, many hunters choose to skin their kill *after* the ageing process.

There are two drawbacks to this: you can't begin to eat all the meat under that hide, and if you want to tan the skin of your creature with the hair on, you will need to remove the hide promptly and get working on it before the hair has any chance to loosen. During warm weather it is also often advisable to skin a creature right away to help the meat cool down. Otherwise this approach is well worth considering.

When is it done ageing?

This is a matter of personal taste and preference. During cool or cold weather, one week is pretty standard practice for most hunters. I have, however, aged meat for more than 40 days during cool weather and been amazed at the results. The complex, unique flavors that evolve over time are comparable to the flavors of high-quality aged cheeses, wines or other well-aged cultured foods. The process of pre-digestion that meat undergoes during an extended ageing also makes it *much* more easy to digest, to the point that some decry it as a curative superfood. All I know is that under ideal conditions (cold and dry) it just keeps on getting better and better until, eventually, it dries solid and becomes a kind of unsalted cured meat. If you plan to age meat for more than 14 days, I suggest skinning it so that it can have more air flow during the extended process.

Having said all of that, for most palates hanging meat *five to fourteen days* will noticeably improve the taste, texture and digestibility of it. *Shorter if it's warm out.*

If you skinned your meat before hanging, it will have likely formed a hard outer rind or film of scum, depending on the humidity. This scum is healthy and normal; it can be scraped off easily with a knife blade held at a right angle to the meat's surface. The outer rind can likewise be trimmed off and used as stew meat.

Scent glands

Before going any further, I should mention the tarsal glands, usually referred to as "scent glands." These glands, mentioned earlier in a couple different contexts, are located in the inside of the legs, around the knee joint. There will usually be a patch of discolored hair marking their exact location. When skinning and butchering, be aware that these glands emit a strong aroma/flavor that can, if you are careless, get on your knife and then be transferred onto meat. This is really not the end of the world, but it is also quite avoidable. Simply wash your knife well if it comes into contact with that area, or switch knifes entirely. Some folks tie a piece of cloth or place a patch of tape over the glands while they are working, to really ensure there is no contamination.

Breaking down the body

The directions that follow are for creatures deer-sized and larger:

Once you've hung and skinned your kill, it's time to butcher it—break it down into smaller sections which will have different uses and can be preserved separately.

The dotted lines show where to cut to remove the head and lower legs, which requires some twisting, finessing and snapping.

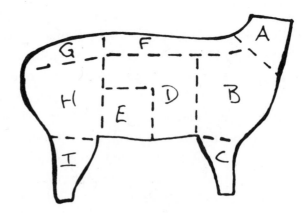

Deer anatomy, showing placement of various cuts: A) neck;
B) shoulder/chuck; C) shank; D) breast/brisket; E) flank;
F) backstrap; G) rump; H) round; I) shank

Quartering

For larger creatures this process sometimes begins with quartering the carcass, which means literally cutting the body into four sections. This is usually accomplished with a fine-toothed saw (a meat saw, hacksaw or electric saw). For creatures the size of moose and elk quartering is often necessary just to pick the carcass up and transport it; for deer-sized animals, it is often unnecessary.

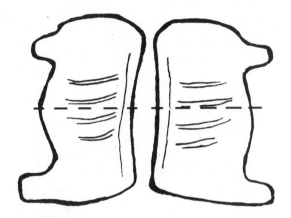

Quartering a carcass. In the illustration, the carcass has been split down the spine. The dotted lines indicate where it would be further cut to separate it into four quarters.

Removing the legs

If you are not quartering the animal—which, as stated above, is often unnecessary—you can begin by removing the legs. The front legs are not actually connected by any bone, just by muscle and connective tissue lying between the shoulder blade and rib cage. Pull the front leg out away from the body and use your knife to find the sweet spot where it will naturally separate from the body, with the assistance of your knife's blade of course.

The hind legs are not quite as easy to remove as a ball-and-socket joint connects them to the pelvis. By cutting around the base of the leg where it meets the body, you will get down to this joint and be able to cut the tendons and tissue holding it together.

Backstraps

With the legs removed, the next big slabs of meat to get are the *backstraps*: two long muscles that run along either side of the spine. These are excellent cuts, and well worth removing carefully. Make a cut alongside the spine, all the way from the neck to the rump. Use your blade to cut right alongside the backbone, first as it descends in toward the ribcage and then out toward the side of the body. Use your hands to feel out the muscle running along the spine; you'll find a distinct, thick "strap" of muscle running along the backbone. Continue cutting close to the bone the muscle is nestled against to free it.

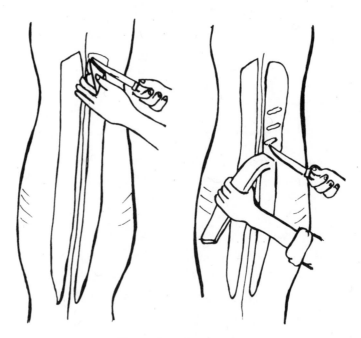

Removing a backstrap.

Tenderloins

The tenderloins are two strips of muscle that lie inside the abdominal cavity, just above where the kidneys once were. They look like mini backstraps and are praised, for good reason, as one of the most tender, delicious cuts. They can be easily removed by pulling and a little coaxing with your knife.

Breast meat or brisket

There will be layers of muscle on the chest that should now be cut off. This is the breast meat or *brisket*, which can add up to a good amount of flesh when it is all removed.

Flank

The abdominal muscle that extends down from the base of the rib-cage toward the pelvis is called the *flank*. It can be easily cut off and should be saved.

Ribs

The ribs of many larger animals are excellent eating. They are usually sawed into sections using a fine-toothed meat saw or hacksaw. An alternative way to deal with ribs is to cut all the meat in between them off, more or less cleaning the ribcage of flesh, and use this as grinding or stew meat.

Neck

The neck of larger animals has a considerable amount of meat on it and shouldn't be overlooked. The head can be removed from its upper end using your knife. At the junction where head and neck meet, cut down to the ball and socket joint and, after cutting through all the connective muscle and tendon, twist the head off. The same basic technique is applied at the other end of the neck: cutting down to the vertebra, detaching as much muscle and tendon as you can, then twisting it off.

Breaking it down further

Once you've sectioned and begun removing the meat from a carcass, you'll want to break it down further. The legs, in particular, will need to be broken down.

The front legs

The meat of the upper front leg is deboned simply by cutting cleanly against the shoulder blade, removing all muscle from it. The lower section of the leg is similarly deboned, as is the shank. The meat on the shank is more sinewy and should be kept apart from that of the upper leg, for use as stewing or grinding meat.

The hind legs

The hind legs are butchered by cutting down to the bone and then freeing the meat from it. By following the natural divisions between the various muscles one can break the hind leg down into smaller roasts, which can then be sliced for drying, frozen as roasts, cut up and frozen as steaks or chopped into stew meat.

What to do with it all

These various muscles and cuts all have different properties that make them suitable for different methods of preparation. Below is a list of the general uses for each cut:

- *Tenderloin:* Steak or medallions. Don't grind, dry or stew this meat; it doesn't need much in the way of adulteration.
- *Backstrap:* Like the tenderloin, backstrap is a very nice cut that can be prepared as steak, sliced thin and added to stir fries and soups or served as venison sashimi. It can be nice dried as jerky, too, since it makes such long, tender strips.
- *Rump:* Roasts, steaks, jerky, stir fry.
- *Round:* Roasts, steaks, jerky, stew, stir fry.
- *Shoulder/Chuck:* Jerky, stew meat, ground, roasts.
- *Breast/Brisket:* This meat can vary quite a bit depending on the size and age of an animal, but is generally tough and can be best used in ground meat, stew meat or dried as jerky and used to make pemmican.
- *Flank:* Generally the same as breast.
- *Neck:* The neck can be roasted whole for a nice feast. The meat can also be cut off and used in the same way as breast meat, but a neck roast is really quite enjoyable.
- *Shank:* Ground meat, stew, braising.

Smaller animals

The process of butchering smaller creatures is similar to that described above, just scaled down and simplified. Don't bother trying to remove the tenderloins or butcher the legs of a squirrel. Instead, just use a good knife to quarter the body or otherwise break it into sections before preparing.

10

Using It All

THE MOST FUNDAMENTAL WAY to honor the life of your prey, the creature whose life you have taken to nourish your own, is by eating its body and treating every part of it as something precious. When we make the fullest use of the animals we kill, we fulfil the alchemical cycle in which death is transformed into life. It is as if there were an invisible contract between hunter and prey, one that every hunter feels intuitively in their bones: that to kill something and waste it is not right.

Beyond this deep imperative to make use of the whole body, there is also the simple fact that you get a lot more food out of the life you have ended by being resourceful and using it all. I have observed that just by eating the organs, rendering the fat, using all the scraps of meat and making rich broths from the bones of a deer, I get considerably more food value out of its carcass than if I only ate the convenient muscle meat. That's nothing to scoff at. What this means is that by fully exploiting all that is available on a creature's body, one can dramatically reduce the amount of life one needs to take, while increasing the amount, diversity and nutrition of the food that life provides. A lighter footprint on the land and a more conscious relationship with one's food is the result.

Of course, perhaps the most enticing motivation I can offer to "use it all" is this: it's fun and it's good for you. Experimenting with new flavors and new foods is tons of fun. I get a huge kick out of serving a group of friends blueberry Jell-O I made myself from scratch out of deerskin, or making a rich testicle broth to serve on a special dinner date. What makes such dishes all the more fun is that they actually taste really good and are incredibly nutritious; more so than most all of the modern, conventional foods we are accustomed to. In various places across the world most of the obscure foods listed below are still consumed as delicacies. The animals we kill for the table hold some of the most wholesome, powerful, nutrient-dense foods one can obtain. It is up to the hunter to recognize and use this nourishment rather than simply taking the meat and leaving the rest to the crows.

The creatures we hunt also provide many incredible gifts that lie outside of the realm of food. From their skins we can make warm clothing, glue, rawhide, instruments and much more. Whole cultures have been built upon tools, transportation and housing derived from the bodies of their prey. To not look into some of these uses and at least dabble in them (or find someone who would like your deerskin, if you don't have the time or it's just not for you) would be a waste, too.

What follows is a comprehensive catalogue of different body parts and their uses. I have included information on handling, preparation, nutrition, traditional uses and medicinal properties where each applies and space allows. It should provide plenty of guidance and suggestions to help you fully honor the body of a creature the best that you can.

Adrenal gland

The adrenal glands are situated just above the kidneys, in a ball of fat that connects them to that organ. To find the adrenals, remove the kidneys when gutting and put them aside. The kidneys are often-times surrounded by a layer of fat, and it is within this layer, just above the kidney itself, that you will find the tiny "adrenaline pearl" hiding. It will usually be in a ball of fat.

Although the adrenal glands are relatively small (usually about the size of a pea or smaller in an adult deer), they contain big nourishment. With allegedly the highest concentration of vitamin C in any animal or plant tissue, the adrenals were traditionally coveted as a potent safeguard against scurvy. Weston Price writes in his pioneering work *Nutrition and Physical Degeneration*:

> When I asked an old Indian, through an interpreter, why the Indians did not get scurvy, he replied promptly that that was a white man's disease.... He then described how when the Indian kills a moose he opens it up and at the back of the moose just above the kidney there are what he described as two small balls in the fat. These he said the Indian would take and cut up into as many pieces as there were little and big Indians in the family and each one would eat his piece.... By eating these foods the Indians would keep free from scurvy.

Although most of us today aren't at risk of developing scurvy, the high levels of organic vitamin C and other nutrients in the adrenal glands are as important now as they ever were.

The adrenal glands are tiny little jewels of powerful, stimulating nutrition. Too small to be a stand-alone snack, they can be added to soups, prepared with the kidneys or eaten as a superfood supplement.

If you want to preserve their high vitamin C content they should be eaten uncooked.

Antler

Antler has probably been used as a rejuvenative, strengthening medicine by many far-flung cultures ever since humans began chopping things up, putting them in hot water and drinking the resultant brew. As the symbolism of the antler might suggest, it has been esteemed as a powerful tonic, often, though by no means exclusively, taken for its fortifying effect on the reproductive system.

Deer, along with elk, moose, caribou and various other ruminants, grow and shed a new set of antlers every year, consuming an enormous amount of energy and nutrients. As mentioned earlier, a buck's annual growth of antlers consumes the same amount of minerals as a pregnant doe needs to form a full-sized fetus inside her womb. That's a lot of energy! Antlers use so many resources because they are far denser than bone. They are not hollow—there is no cavity for marrow in their center—and are extremely hard. Antlers have been used traditionally as tools in preference to bone for this reason.

Before the antler has fully formed and ossified (turned into bone), one can extract some of this dense mineral content. Traditional medicinal uses of antler include:
- Treating arthritis and sore joints;
- Increasing physical/athletic endurance;
- Countering tooth decay;
- Increasing libido/fertility;
- Stimulating circulation;
- Stimulating tissue regeneration;
- A general strengthening nutritive tonic.

Antlers are used for their medicinal properties when they are young and growing, while they are still covered in the brown velvet fuzz that coats them in the early to late summer months. Traditionally the whole growing antler from bucks killed in mid-summer was used. During these months the antler is soft enough to cut through with a knife like a potato, so it can be simply chopped up and dried for future use. Apparently even fully mature, ossified antlers were used traditionally as a lower-grade product. These would be sawed up (a hacksaw works well) or otherwise cut into small pieces and simmered for many hours into a broth.

The velvet fur coating the antler also has medicinal properties (in fact all modern antler health supplements are made from it). If you kill a deer in late summer or early fall and its antlers are still coated with this velvet, scrape or cut it off with a knife and dry it for future use.

Antler tea

Dried antler velvet, or whole slices of antler that have been dried, can be made into a tea by adding one tablespoon of dried antler material to one quart of water and simmering for 15 to 30 minutes. This is a serious brew best taken by people who are somewhat depleted or have a condition that really calls for the building, nourishing medicine of antler.

Antler tincture

Antler can also be prepared as a tincture. In a canning jar pour your choice of distilled liquor (40 percent or higher alcohol content) over dried antler velvet, with a ratio of one part dried antler to two parts liquid. Let sit at least six weeks, agitating the jar every couple days to help the extraction process. After the minimum six weeks, strain and use as a supplement, taking a couple drops a day as needed.

Antler broth

Antler can also be used as an addition to any stock you make. Simply toss in some sliced or sawed pieces of antler with whatever bones you are making stock out of, for some extra oomph.

Blood

Blood from a healthy, happy creature is an amazing and powerful food. Although rarely featured in standard modern diets, blood has been enjoyed for its wonderful flavor and delicate texture for millennia. Masai herders traditionally consumed blood mixed with milk as a dietary staple. Mongolian warriors would supposedly carefully draw blood from their horses in order to have a nutrient-dense food while at battle. Blood pudding and blood sausage are still dietary mainstays in some parts of the world.

When you kill a creature using an arrow or bullet, it typically dies by bleeding. This means that when you come upon the dead body, slitting its throat will not produce a gushing stream of blood; the heart has stopped pumping, and has already pumped out some of the body's reserves from being wounded. Still, there is much blood that can be found.

When you are gutting, if you do a clean job and avoid perforating the stomach and intestines, a quantity of blood will usually remain pooled in the cavity where the organs were—scoop it out into a clean container and save it. Pump blood out of the heart with your hands into this container. Pumping the limbs may also produce more blood that has been pooling in the ribcage.

Blood clots very quickly upon contact with oxygen. This is okay—it even makes the blood easier to collect and move, coagulating into big slippery globs that can be picked up. If you would like to prevent clotting, however, you can do so by adding some vinegar to the blood right away. I have used approximately a third of cup of vinegar to four cups of blood successfully.

If you are thawing frozen meat, blood often pools in whatever dish you put under it as it defrosts, ready to use.

Now that you have some blood, it's time to figure out how to use it.

Dried blood

Blood can be preserved by drying, which is incredibly simple: just put it into a ceramic bowl or glass dish and wait for the water in it to evaporate. A warmer place of course speeds up this process, full sun being ideal. In my experience flies are not at all interested in blood; they will not touch it or lay eggs on it.

When the blood is done drying it will have turned dark and solid, so you'll have to break it off of the dish you dried it on in chunks. Eat it in whole chunks or as a powder added to other foods—it can

Dried blood.

stick to your teeth, so I like to suck on it or eat it powdered. This is a great blood-building supplement, containing loads of zinc, iron, B vitamins and many nutrients.

Recipe ideas

When cooked, blood thickens, turns a dark, greyish color, and takes on a pleasant, smooth, soft texture and a delicious, subtle, meaty flavor.

It can be cooked in a pan along with chopped onions, tender chunks of meat and vegetables to make a "blood hash," added to haggis or ground meat, incorporated into soups (blood treated with vinegar is usually used for this) or prepared as the traditional blood sausage.

Blood sausage

This is an old recipe for blood sausage a friend shared with me that doesn't contain any grain, which many will appreciate.

Ingredients

- 2 cups fresh blood
- 1 lb fresh animal fat (tallow or suet)
- 2 eggs
- 1 cup chopped onion
- 1 tablespoon butter, tallow or other cooking oil
- ½ teaspoon thyme
- 1 bay leaf
- ground pepper
- Sausage casings

Directions

Cook onions in your preferred oil until tender. Dice fat into half-inch chunks and half melt in a pot. Remove from heat and allow to cool slightly. Mix beaten eggs in and add a pinch of ground pepper and thyme and a bay leaf. Add cooked onions to this mixture, mix well and proceed to add blood and mix.

Fill sausage casings with this mixture until just over three-quarters full, since it will expand during cooking. Plunge these sausages into boiling water, leaving plenty of room for them to expand. Reduce the heat to a simmer and allow to cook 20 minutes before removing. Using a wire basket or steamer to contain them can make removing them easier.

These sausages can be refrigerated or frozen until you want to use them, at which time they can be gently cooked in a pan in oil.

Bone

The bones of any animal killed for food should not be disregarded. They in fact constitute one of the most nourishing and significant parts of a creature's body. Traditional cultures and modern gourmets alike have always prized bone-based broths for their outstanding, complex flavors and amazing health benefits.

There is an old saying that "good broth brings the dead back to life." Bone-based broths are packed with minerals and proteins from the marrow and bone tissue itself, giving the body easily assimilated building blocks, trace minerals and oils that are rarely available in modern foods.

The prime "soup bones" of most mammals are the leg bones, which structurally can be described as long, marrow-filled shafts. The high marrow content of these bones makes them ideal for the stock pot. Other bones vary in their usefulness for broth; ribs, for instance, contain relatively little marrow and are not typically thought of as "soup bones," while the spine can be used to make a rich broth.

Adding a chunk of antler or a couple of hooves, skinned and sawed into chunks, will further enrich a broth.

Bone broth preparation

To prepare bone broth you will need a large stock pot, a heat source and plenty of time.

For small creatures such as rabbits, the whole boney carcass can be thrown into your stock pot as is. With larger creatures, you will sometimes want to crack the bones open. This applies particularly to the leg bones (prime for broth), which can be cracked open with a rock (messy) or sawed into sections at several-inch intervals with a hacksaw (tidy). By breaking or sawing the bone open it's nutrients and oils can be more easily extracted.

Making a rich and satisfying broth from these bones can be as simple as throwing what looks like an adequate amount into your stock pot, covering with water, adding some choice seasonings and letting simmer at a very low heat for 12 to 72 hours. A tablespoon of vinegar is customarily added to any such broth before cooking; it helps draw calcium and other minerals out and into the stock. The best broths also typically contain a couple different types of bone. For example, when using leg bones, be sure to include the knee joints, as the cartilage and inevitable meaty chunks left over on this section add a lot of flavor and nutrition to the stock. Hooves are also added for their rich gelatin content, automatically making any broth much richer, more nourishing and satisfying.

The tried and true recipe below produces outstanding broths without fail.

Miles' favorite deer bone broth ──────────

Ingredients
- Bones from 2 deer legs, sawed open/into sections
- 2 deer hooves, skinned, and any attached bone shaft sawed open into sections

- Section of antler, cut into sections with hacksaw (optional)
    - 3 onions, skin removed, chopped in half
    - 3 carrots, whole
    - 3 cloves garlic, whole, unpeeled
    - 1 tablespoon vinegar
    - 4 to 8 quarts water

Directions

Combine first six ingredients in stock pot, add vinegar and cover with water. Bring to a boil, then reduce to a low heat, keeping the broth at a gentle simmer. Allow to brew at least 12 hours, and up to 72 hours. Occasionally check the stock to see if too much water has evaporated. Add water if needed.

When done brewing, strain and allow to cool. A layer of fat will rise to the surface and harden. If you like a greasy broth, leave this. If you don't, remove but keep this fat. It is marrow fat, an extremely healthy, delicious and useful oil (see the Marrow section later in this chapter for more).

You now have an incredible base for soups, sauces or whatever else calls for a rich, flavorful broth. It can be stored in containers in the freezer or incorporated into meals and eaten up before it has the chance to go bad.

For smaller-boned creatures (rabbit, grouse, etc.), simmering the whole bone-carcass 6 hours is usually sufficient to make a rich broth.

Brain

Brains have traditionally been fed to babies to help improve their memory—they are of course the original "brain food." They are quite delicious, with a flavor reminiscent of the best farm-fresh eggs. Brain tacos are still a popular food with some.

Remove brains from the skull either the messy way—by smashing it open with a rock—or more cleanly using a saw to cut a V-shaped notch on the forehead, which can be knocked out to open it up. The brains are then scooped out.

The simplest way to prepare brains for the table is to sauté them; the result is comparable to scrambled egg yolks, but with a richer flavor and a pleasant, delicate texture.

Diaphragm

The diaphragm is a thin muscle attached all around the ribcage, separating the lungs and heart from the digestive organs below. When gutting, you will have to remove this muscle along with everything else. Keep it. It is a great, useable chunk of meat! I tossed it away for years until a friend stopped me and explained the obvious: it's edible muscle meat. Use it as stew meat or grind it.

Eye

Eyes don't represent a very substantial proportion of any creature's body. They do, however, represent a disproportionately dense concentration of minerals and other nutrients. Zinc, for instance, is more concentrated in eye tissue than anywhere else in the body. Eyes, coincidentally, require large amounts of zinc to function optimally; this of course means that eyeballs are eye food. Don't neglect them!

If you are making a broth out of the head, you are already getting these nutrients. If not, consider removing the eyes with your knife and either adding them to a soup or some ground meat.

A tray of dried salmon eyes.

Eyes can also be dried. Fish eyes in particular are tasty dried: a salty, crispy snack. Simply place eyeballs on a screen someplace warm or in your dehydrator and remove when hard.

The degeneration of eyesight has become something of an expected norm in our culture, meaning that everyone would probably benefit from nutritional prophylactics like this.

Fat

Body fat can be rendered into an extremely stable, healthy oil ideal for cooking, baking, soap making and many other uses. There are two kinds of fat one will encounter: subcutaneous fat or tallow, which lies just beneath the skin and provides a kind of insulation to the body; and visceral fat or suet, which surrounds the stomach, intestines and organs, providing a protective covering around them. There are slight differences in the nutritional qualities of these two fats (the visceral fat contains special antimicrobial, healing properties), but for all practical purposes they are the same.

If you encounter a substantial amount of visceral fat when gutting the animal, be sure to save it. After skinning the carcass, if there is a substantial amount of subcutaneous fat, you will be able to trim it off with your knife, sometimes getting nice slabs of pure fat. You can freeze this fat until you are ready to process it.

Rendering fat

Rendering fat is a process by which the pure oil is extracted from the protein tissue using heat.

To render fat you will need a pot, a wooden spoon or stirring stick and some patience. Begin with a modest-sized batch, working with maybe a few pounds of fat.

Chop fat into approximately one-inch to half-inch cubes. No need to be too particular here; the goal is just to reduce the size of each piece so that the oil can be extracted more easily and evenly.

Place chopped fat into a pot and put over a low heat. For the first 10 to 20 minutes you will want to keep an eye on your rendering fat, stirring it occasionally as needed to ensure that it is not sticking to the pot. This initial phase is the most critical part of the process, as if the fat sticks and burns, this will affect the quality of the final product, so keep an eye on the pot and keep the fat moving periodically.

As the fat heats up and you stir it, you will see that it is releasing pure oil. Eventually it will release enough of its own oil that it begins to drown in it. At this point the danger of the fat sticking and burning is reduced considerably and you can stir it less frequently. Eventually the solid chunks of fat will be more or less floating in liquid oil. They will shrink as this liquid oil is extracted from them, to the point that when you remove a shriveled chunk from the pot of gently bubbling liquid, it will be a crispy "craquelin" similar in flavor and texture to a pork rind.

Once you have reached this point, remove fat from heat and allow to cool slightly. Fat at this temperature is dangerously hot to play around with. Strain the still-warm liquid oil into jars or other containers for storage and allow to cool fully (it will become solid or semi-solid) before placing a lid on it; this allows any latent moisture to escape.

You should store your rendered fat in a cool place. It will last many months without going rancid and is a fantastic, healthful oil.

Foot/hoof

The webbed feet of all birds are packed with gelatin and should be saved and used to make a rich broth. Hooves, likewise, make an outstanding broth, and should always be skinned and used for this purpose. See the section on bone broths for more suggestions.

Head

The whole, antlerless head of a deer can be skinned and added to a stock pot to produce a rich, meaty broth. Simmer at least six hours, with seasonings or vegetables of your choosing, before straining. Pick the meat off of the cooked head to add to your soup.

Heart

Of all the organ meats, heart is likely the easiest for most people to embrace. It is after all a muscle, and as such tastes not unlike a very good cut of red meat. It can be prepared any way you would a good, tender cut of muscle meat: slice it into heart steaks and pan fry; chop it into cubes and make "heart kebabs" with your favorite veggies; add cubed heart to soups in the final few minutes of cooking; marinate, slice thinly and dry it into a special heart jerky.

The heart can also be stuffed with garlic or apple slices and roasted whole in an oven. Then cool and slice the roasted heart as a kind of delicious natural lunch meat.

Although it tastes similar to muscle meat, heart has a distinctive, pleasant texture all its own and contains healing properties far more powerful than any other muscle in the body. It is a source of unique and uncommon vitamins, trace minerals, enzymes and proteins.

Like other organs, the heart is often surrounded by a layer of clear connective tissue that is chewy and tough. Remove this layer, if it is apparent, before cutting up and preparing the heart.

Intestine

The most significant use of intestine is of course as sausage casing. There are accounts of indigenous people eating sections of the small intestine with pre-digested food still in them. I tried this once, but wasn't able to keep it down; it tasted too much like shit. Literally.

To prepare intestine for use as a sausage casing, begin by cutting a section and emptying it (during the rut, bucks may conveniently not have anything in their intestines to begin with). I have only tried this with the small intestine, which has a smaller and more uniform diameter than the large intestine. Use a hose or faucet, and a funnel if needed, to flush the intestine well, until the water coming out one end is clear. If you can enlist someone to help you, it will make this process much more graceful. Having one person hold up a section of intestine while the other makes sure the water is going in and massages it through works well. Remove any fat or other material from the outside of the intestine at this time, also.

You will now want to turn the intestines inside out. To do this, fold one end up like the cuff of a sleeve, and keep on moving it upward. Once you get going with it a basic method will develop.

Rub the now inverted intestines with some coarse salt, and rinse again. In a large bowl, pot or bucket, mix together some salt water and add some chopped onion to it. Place the thoroughly cleaned intestines into this brine and allow to sit in it overnight, someplace cool. This will remove any odors and impurities. After all this cleaning and soaking, they are ready to be used (or refrigerated/frozen until that time comes).

Kidney

Kidneys are one of the most nutritious of the organ meats. They should be used as fresh as possible. They are usually covered in a layer of fat; this kidney fat is extremely nutritious and should be saved for rendering or eating. After peeling away the fat coating them, there is a transparent layer of connective tissue that should be removed. Slice this layer with your knife, then use your fingers to peel it off. At this point many like to cut the kidneys in half, or slice them into quarter- or half-inch rounds and soak in salt water for a few hours. This mellows the flavor.

After soaking, the kidneys can be prepared any number of ways. One can sear them in a pan with butter, as halves or sliced.

Liver

The liver, like the kidneys and all of the other tender internal organs, should be used while it is still fresh, or kept very cold/frozen. Like the kidneys, it is also covered by a thin transparent filament. Remove this by making a slice with a blade and then using your hands to peel it off.

Liver can be seared, pan cooked with onions, made into delicious pâtés or even sliced into thin strips and dried; it makes a surprisingly sweet and extremely nourishing jerky.

Lung

Lungs are rarely thought of as an edible organ meat today, but have featured prominently in many traditional cuisines. The famed Scottish haggis often includes lung, and the indigenous people of the Great Plains region would traditionally eat bison lung dried. The lungs constitute one of the largest internal organs, so to simply discard them in the bush is to overlook a substantial gift of nourishment.

To dry lung, slice into thin, long strips, marinate (if you wish), and otherwise prepare as you would any jerky. Dried lung has a light, fluffy texture that is almost comparable to popcorn and a mellow, pleasant flavor.

Lungs can alternatively be boiled in water for 40 minutes (or until fully cooked through), put through a meat grinder, and then used as part of a filling for sausages (along with other ground meats, fat, spices and seasonings), as a nutritious supplement mixed into ground meat (this, often called "mystery meat," is a great way of getting picky eaters to eat organ meats) or as an ingredient in haggis (described later in this chapter).

Marrow

Bone marrow is pure delicious fat; chock full of growth-promoting stem cells, essential fatty acids and minerals, it should not be overlooked.

The long, hollow leg bones contain the most easily accessed marrow. This can be removed fresh by cracking the leg bones open using a rock or other hard, blunt instrument. Fresh marrow is considered an extremely healing food, stimulating cell regeneration. You can store it in a container in the fridge and eat a small piece daily as a strengthening natural supplement.

Extracting bone marrow.

Marrow can also be rendered for longer-term storage. This can be as simple as skimming the layer of fat that rises and solidifies at the surface of bone broth when it cools. This is pure marrow fat. If you'd like to store it for any length of time, place this rendered marrow into a pot and bring to a low heat. Let sit at this low heat for at least ten minutes; this will ensure that any water is removed from the fat, so what you are left with will not go rancid quickly. Store in jars in a cool place and use as you would butter, lard or tallow.

Traditionally the leg bones of creatures would be put into large pots, covered with water, simmered for an hour then cooled. The fat that rose to the top would be removed and then gently heated. This has served as the primary dietary oil for many hunting cultures.

Pancreas

The pancreas, which also goes by the culinary term "sweetbreads," is a glandular organ located just below the stomach of mammals. As the name "sweetbreads" suggests, pancreas has a mild, enjoyable flavor and a light, fluffy texture. I'm almost afraid to say it, but this is an instance where the old saying "it tastes like chicken" is actually somewhat true. Pan-cooked sweetbreads are a light meat with a gentle flavor similar to chicken.

Pancreas is, however, much more nutritious than chicken breast. It is incredibly high in a number of vitamins and minerals, including zinc and vitamins B_{12}, C and K_2, a kind of supervitamin found in some organ meats that has been used to halt and even reverse tooth decay. And it tastes good; even those with an unadventurous palate are often able to enthusiastically get behind sweetbreads.

Sauté or pan fry sweetbreads with whatever flavor you like—they are delicious.

Sinew

Sinew is a term used in reference to long tendons. These tendons can be extracted from the body, dried and separated into thin strands for a multitude of uses, including: natural sewing thread; twisted into extremely strong cord, bowstrings and snares; as a traditional backing material to add strength to bows.

The most useable pieces of sinew are found as a flat, silver sheet running along either side of the spine, and as a strong tendon running up the back side of the lower leg.

Dry sinew out in a warm location against a flat board (so it dries flat). To prepare it for use, pull strips of backstrap sinew apart into individual threads using your fingernails/hands. The leg sinew, however, needs to be gently pounded between rocks in order to get it to separate into individual strands. Emphasis on *gentle*; you don't want to destroy the sinew, only pound it well enough that it will separate to the point that the long individual strands can be separated.

Sinew has a well-deserved reputation for being incredibly strong, but it should be noted that it gets very slippery, stretchy and weak when wet. Use it only for projects that won't involve much contact with water.

For the food uses of sinew see Tendon, later in this chapter.

Skin

To fully explore the many uses of skin is well beyond the scope of this book. From buckskin to rawhide to bark-tanned leather to hide glue to Jell-O, it would take several books to fully do the subject justice. Fortunately, some of those books exist (see the Resources section at the end of this book). I have included some basic instructions on dealing with a hide in Chapter 8: Skinning, though. And of course I have to include a recipe here for what is by far my favorite use of skin: the delicious, wholesome dessert known as Jell-O.

Jell-O, as you may or may not know, is actually made out of pig skins. It is basically an aqueous extract of collagen, the main protein that forms skin, which below a certain temperature gels (due to its gelatin content) into the dessert we know and love.

To prepare Jell-O from your deerskin (or moose, elk, etc.), you will first want to transform it into rawhide, which is just a hide that you have scraped the flesh and hair off of and dried out. My book *Unlearn, Rewild* has instructions on how to do this, as does Matt Richards' *Deerskins into Buckskins*. Once you have some dry rawhide on hand, you are ready to get started.

Deer skin Jell-O

Ingredients
- 2 cups dried deer rawhide, cut into strips
- 1 gallon water
- Flavoring (e.g., berry juice; dried fruit; whatever you think of)

Directions

Cut rawhide into half-inch strips and place in pot. Add warm water and let skin soak it up for a few hours. Bring to a boil and then reduce to a very low heat, gently simmering/brewing for 4 hours. Make sure the water doesn't completely evaporate, but keep in mind that some water reduction is desirable. If you will be flavoring your Jell-O with some kind of juice, this will allow you to replenish the evaporated water with your flavoring agent. Allow to cool slightly, strain, flavor to taste (adding whole berries or chunks of fruit produces a very nice effect) and chill 6–12 hours or overnight. It will "set" during this time.

The resulting dessert is incredibly delicious, and apparently amazingly healing and soothing to the digestive system, nourishing structural tissues in the body (cartilage, skin, bone, hair, etc.) and much more. In Chinese medicine it is considered one of the most important *yin* tonics; *yin* being the material, structural essence of the body.

Spleen

The spleen is brown, flat, oval-shaped organ comparable in appearance, texture and flavor to liver. It is connected to the upper outside wall of the stomach, which it can be easily peeled off of. Like the liver it is covered in a membrane which should be removed before preparation. The membrane of the spleen is tough enough to make it quite chewy and well worth your time in peeling off, for what lies beneath is very tender.

Prepare as you would liver: as a pâté, ground and added to sausages or regular ground meat, fried with onions, etc. Finely sliced pig's spleen is a traditional soup ingredient in China.

Stomach

Stomach is a renowned feature of many cuisines around the world, either as a feast-sized sausage casing in the famous Scottish haggis (and other lesser-known, similar dishes enjoyed in other cultures) or as the stand-alone tripe enjoyed from China to Nigeria. Cleaned stomachs were also used in days gone by as waterproof containers. For any of these uses a stomach must, first and foremost, be cleaned. There are a couple methods of accomplishing this that I am aware of; here I will describe a procedure that I have successfully employed myself.

Cleaning a deer stomach

Begin by removing any large chunks of fat from the outside of the stomach. Then move on to the task of emptying the stomach. You will have to cut it open somewhere in order to facilitate this; I usually choose to do this at one of the lower ends where it narrows into

A deer stomach turned inside out. After soaking overnight,
the inner membrane can be easily rubbed off with a rag.

a tube (the duodenum). Squeeze all the food out, eventually turning the stomach inside out. It is made of several chambers, which can be a bit confusing (the different chambers are thought to have different culinary properties, but I don't know enough about the subject to comment further). Use a hose or a sink to thoroughly wash the inside-out stomach as well as you can. Now you will want to remove the thin, dark, innermost lining. I have accomplished this by allowing the stomach to soak for one to several days in bucket of water, until this layer loosens and can be removed simply by taking one's hand or a rag and rubbing it off.

Another method of removing this layer is to boil the stomach for an hour, after which it should come off easily. Then soak the stomach in a solution of vinegar and water for at least one hour. This should help remove much of the "digestive" scent and taste. Rinse in fresh water.

Now you have the weaponry to make your own haggis, tripe or a neat container. The haggis recipe below comes from TV chef Hugue Dufour.

Deer haggis

Ingredients

- 1 thoroughly cleaned deer stomach
- Deer lungs, liver, heart, kidney (and/or other organs)
- 4 cups diced onions
- 2 cups diced peeled apples
- 1 cup diced deer fat (unrendered suet or tallow)
- ¼ cup lightly roasted rolled oat flakes
- ¼ cup maple syrup
- A pinch of grated nutmeg
- Butter
- Sauce
- Diced tomatoes
- Deer bone broth (see recipe earlier in this chapter)

Directions

In a large pot cook the cleaned stomach, lungs, liver, kidneys and heart in gently boiling water for two hours. Remove the stomach and organs from the pot and allow to cool.

In a large frying pan, sweat diced onions with butter over a medium heat. When done, put aside. In another pan, cook the apples in butter as well. Add grated nutmeg and maple syrup to this and caramelize for 25 minutes or until done. Put this aside as well.

Use a meat grinder to grind the lungs and other organs as well as the deer fat. Mix the ground organs together in a large bowl, then add the cooked onions, apples and rolled oats. Fill the deer stomach with this mixture. Then tie closed the opening you used to both empty and fill the stomach with a string of strong, natural fibre. Poke small holes in the stomach with a sharp knife.

Poach the now stuffed stomach in hot, but not quite boiling, water for about an hour.

Set oven to 375 degrees.

Remove stomach from poaching water and place it into a large saucepan. Cover the haggis with some of the sauce and pour the rest into the pan. Cook in oven for 40 minutes, basting regularly with the sauce.

Sauce

Combine an equal quantity of diced tomatoes, concentrated meat stock and beef broth. Stir with a hand mixer.

Preparing tripe

To prepare a cleaned stomach for use as tripe, cut it into one-inch squares or strips roughly a quarter of an inch wide by two inches long and boil for 3 hours or until tender. This can now be incorporated into any recipe calling for tripe.

Preparing a stomach container

To make a rot-resistant, waterproof container from a cleaned stomach (do not employ the boiling method of cleaning a stomach if doing this), you will need to "tan" it. This is accomplished by immersing the cleaned, rinsed stomach in a tannin-rich tea made from small, chopped-up chunks of bark from spruce, hemlock, fir, birch or willow trees. The tannins bind with the proteins of the stomach to preserve and strengthen it. Peel bark from living or freshly fallen trees (be sure to take less than a quarter of the tree's diameter worth of bark if you want it to continue a healthy life), chop into small pieces with a hatchet, and simmer in a stock pot with water (one part bark to two parts water) for at least one hour. Allow to cool. Place this tannin tea, along with stomach, in a plastic or wooden container, making sure stomach is fully submerged, and allow to tan for a week. Periodically shift the stomach around to make sure it is not folded in on itself and can absorb the tannin through all of its surfaces. It should get dyed a darker color by the tannin tea. When it is done tanning, remove from tea, stuff with old cloth or something equivalent and allow to dry in this shape.

A deer stomach container, stuffed with
cloth to dry in a full shape.

Tail

You may have heard of the infamous oxtail soup, prepared by simmering the skinned tail of a cow or bull over many hours. This is
a coveted delicacy in Asia, and has been used as a tonifying, healing elixir in traditional Chinese medicine for millennia. Tails, like
hooves and knee joints, are filled with collagen, which is of course
what skin is made of. It comes as no surprise then that tail has been
prized in Asia as a beautifying, skin-toning food.

Although most of the animals one hunts have tails that are considerably shorter than those of cattle (a deer tail might measure seven
inches long, while a cow's tail is typically over a foot in length), they
still are an incredible food source and should not be overlooked. Be
sure to cleanly remove the skin after you remove the tail with your
knife. To make "ox-tail soup" from this tail, you can chop it up or add
it whole to the stock pot, cover with four quarts of water and bring
to a low simmer for at least six hours. A variety of vegetables and
herbs can be added with the tail when making this broth—see the
earlier section on bone broths for ideas. After the broth has cooked

an adequate time, it can be strained for use or soup ingredients can be added directly to it, with the tail left in.

You will be shocked at how rich and gelatinous a stock a relatively small deer's tail will produce. Tail soup is not only reputed to be an deeply healing, nourishing, strengthening food, it *feels* very strongly like all of those things. The perfect fortifying meal for a cold winter day.

Tendon

Tendon is not a common Western food, but is a delicious and prominent feature in many Asian cuisines. From Vietnamese tendon soup to the traditional Chinese appetizer of tender, well-cooked beef tendon served cold, there are numerous ways of preparing this nourishing delicacy. Like hooves, tails and skin, tendon is loaded with collagen and other proteins that nourish the skin, bones, cartilage, hair and tendons.

The main tendons used for the table are located along the back side of the lower legs. These should be cut off and put aside when butchering, and can be frozen until you are ready to prepare them, or dried and then rehydrated before use (by soaking in water overnight).

Preparing tendon

Tendon needs to be cooked for many hours in order to render it tender and appealing. You can add it to a pot of broth for a long slow cook, cook it by itself and eat it sliced and seasoned as a stand-alone dish or add it pre-cooked and sliced into soups. What follows are instructions for one method of cooking tendon by itself.

Rinse tendon under cold water and then place in a pot with a steamer insert. Add water (and an optional quarter cup of soy sauce) to partially cover tendons. Bring the liquid to a boil and then reduce to a simmer and allow to cook for four hours. Add more water as needed, ensuring that the pot does not completely dry out.

The lower leg of a deer has a thick band of
tendon that runs along its back side. In this
photo the tendon has been partially cut off,
to show how it is connected and removed.

Remove tendons from the pot and allow to cool. They can be
stored in a refrigerator for a week or longer. When cold, cut the tendon into ⅛-inch-thick slices, which can then be added to soups and
stews or served alone.

As a stand-alone appetizer, a traditional Chinese method is to
mix tendon with some good vinegar, soy sauce and other seasonings
of your choice (chili oil, salt and chopped green onion and cilantro,
for instance). Allow the tendon to sit for an hour or two at room
temperature in this dressing, fully absorbing all the flavors, before
serving as a cold dish.

Testicle

For anyone who hasn't eaten testicle, the thought of doing so probably evokes giggles and joking; for anyone who has, it likely evokes fond memories of a delicious, rare delicacy. Testicles have a fantastic, salty flavor and a texture not all that different from hot dogs. To procure them, slice the scrotum open and remove. The testicles are covered in a very tough layer of clear tissue; to remove this make an incision in it and peel off using your fingers.

Testicles are fantastic grilled over an open flame; like hot dogs or smokies they will swell and their outer skin will break. Grilled testicles can be eaten as is.

Testicles also make a wonderful broth. To prepare "balls broth," chop testicles finely and add to a pot. Cover with two to three quarts of water and bring to a low simmer for at least one hour. Use this as a tasty, nutritious soup base, preferably leaving the tender chunks of testicle in.

If like nourishes like, it goes without saying that testicles are beneficial to the male reproductive system.

Thymus

The thymus gland and pancreas both share the nickname "sweetbreads." The pancreas is often called belly sweetbreads, and the thymus is called throat sweetbreads. The thymus is located in the upper chest, just behind the breastbone and below the collarbone.

Throat sweetbreads are prepared in much the same way pancreas/belly sweetbreads are, and are generally considered to be of a slightly finer flavor and texture than their lower counterpart (pancreas).

Tongue

Tongue is in texture and flavor closer to heart than any other meat. Some say this is because the tongue is actually attached to the heart by a series of ligaments. I don't know if this is true, but anyone who has tasted the two meats would say it sounds about right. Tongues are rich in healthy oils; in fact there are records of indigenous hunters in the Canadian north killing caribou and *only* taking the tongues, so esteemed was it as a food. That is of course a disgusting way to treat a prey animal, but goes to show that there is something special about tongue.

There is a thick rind surrounding the tongue that should be removed before eating. This is accomplished by cooking in hot water or broth. Using broth or adding an onion and some garlic, salt and herbs will impart some nice flavors to the tongue. A deer tongue should be simmered in this liquid for an hour or two, then removed and allowed to cool. Larger tongues (from moose or elk) should be simmered for a few hours; the tough outer covering will then easily peel off. The tongue can now be prepared any number of ways: sliced and fried; chopped and added to salad; served cold, sliced like a sandwich meat (a North American tradition); added to soups, sliced; or chopped up and stir fried.

In Mexico seasoned, fried tongue is a choice taco stuffing. The most common method of preparation in North America is as "tongue toast"—an open-faced sandwich comprised of a slice of toast, atop which butter and cooked, sliced tongue is placed.

Ulna

The ulna is a thin leg bone attached by connective tissue to the radius. On its own it makes a very handy little bone knife, which can be really useful in gutting small fish and other lightweight applications.

To separate the ulna/radius, allow it to sit out, someplace where it will stay moist (possibly buried), until the connective tissue holding the two bones together weakens. Once that the ulna is free, you might want to wash it with some hot soapy water. After you have sharpened it, grinding it against any natural, abrasive stone you find to give it a sharper edge, it is ready for action.

Windpipe

The windpipe from any creature of deer size or greater makes a handy blow-tube, typically used for blowing on the embers of a fire from a safe distance. If you are a camper or regularly have outdoor fires, this is something you will appreciate. Let it dry in the sun or some other warm place. Try and avoid getting it wet, or be sure to dry it out well if you do; if moist for too long it will begin to decay.

11

Preservation

PRESERVING ONE'S KILL can sometimes be as much of an art and take as much work as the hunt itself. Without thinking ahead and ensuring you have a plan for how you are actually going to deal with your harvest, a successful hunt can easily become a stressful and potentially wasteful mistake. The story related earlier of Christopher McCandless and the cow moose is a dramatic example of this.

Of course most people reading this will have freezers, which automatically make preserving things like meat, fat, bones and hides a simple affair. In some situations, however, other methods of preservation might be more desirable or necessary. I have personally lived for many years without a freezer or electricity, a situation that forced me to experiment with a variety of other, traditional methods of preservation. Regardless of where or how you live, sometimes venison jerky is just appealing; it is after all one of the most delicious ways of preparing wild meat. Or perhaps you don't have space to keep a whole deer, elk or moose in your freezer, or don't even have space for a freezer at all.

What follows is a collection of different ways to preserve your harvest, ranging from the most simple and modern techniques to more traditional, low-tech and even archaic ones.

Freezing

Freezing meat can be as easy as putting it into a bag or wrapping it in butcher paper and throwing it into your freezer. There are, however, simple ways of packing and treating it that will greatly extend the time it can be frozen without suffering freezer burn.

Create an oxygen-free environment

Vacuum-sealed packaging is often considered the best way of packing meat that will be frozen for any length of time. Removing all the oxygen protects the meat from the main element that causes it to degrade or "burn." A vacuum packer may be the right tool for you, but a decent-quality one is an expensive piece of equipment, and you will also need special non-reusable plastic packages in order to use it. A simple, equally effective alternative can be fashioned using nothing more than plastic ziplock freezer bags and water. Simply put your meat into the freezer bag, fill the bag with cold water (that is, *really* cold water) and shake it to make any air bubbles float to the surface. Then squeeze the bag slightly so that water begins to spill out, and seal it. What the vacuum sealer does through suction the water accomplishes by displacement. Very small creatures can be frozen whole in this way. Using this method, birds will keep for up to six months without degrading, and red meat for up to a year.

Freeze it fast

The other main factor that can affect the quality of your frozen meat is the amount of time it takes to freeze once you have put it into the freezer. The slower something freezes, the larger the ice crystals that form; large ice crystals damage the cell walls of the muscle tissue and change the texture and flavor of the meat. To freeze things quickly, spread your packages of meat with about two inches of space between them. Once they have frozen you can stack them up and store them all together, but allowing them room for air to circulate around them during the freezing phase will ensure they freeze as fast as possible with little if any effect on the quality of the meat.

But don't freeze it too fast

A word of caution: don't freeze any meat until a minimum of 24–48 hours has passed since it was killed. This time allows a bit of ageing/ enzymatic breakdown to occur, improving the quality of the meat considerably. So don't rush here.

Drying

Drying is likely the oldest method of preserving meat, and depending on your tastes, one of the most delicious. The basic principle is to slice lean meat into quarter-inch-thick strips, so that moisture can easily and evenly escape, and then put it someplace well ventilated and warm to dry. I should emphasize *lean* here, as any fat on your jerky will go rancid quickly, whereas lean meat alone can be preserved for many months simply by drying. So cut away any chunks of fat. Wild meat from animals like deer, moose and elk is rarely ever marbled with fat, which makes it ideal for jerky. To make your jerky more tender and delicate, slice it against the grain of the meat.

The actual drying can be accomplished by hanging strips in the sun and wind, above or beside a furnace or wood stove, in a dehydrator or in an oven. The benefits of an oven or dehydrator are that the meat takes up little space and is protected from flies and other hungry critters, and one has complete control over the temperature. An oven cooks the meat, too. The benefit of hanging meat to dry, whether outdoors or in, is that one can actually preserve a large amount of meat at once this way. A dehydrator or oven have a very limited capacity in comparison.

Using a dehydrator or oven

To dry meat in a dehydrator, slice strips of meat roughly a quarter inch thick and as long as you can. Season as you like. Lay on racks and turn to the highest heat setting. If you marinate your strips before putting them into the dehydrator, be sure to get a good deal of the moisture off of them before you put them in to dry.

To dry using an oven, place strips on baking sheets or directly on oven racks (with a sheet of foil beneath to catch drippings) and set the oven temperature to 160 degrees. The meat will be dry in six to eight hours. Half way through this period, flip the strips over. They are done when they have darkened and break when bent.

Drying outdoors, or indoors with a heat source

For drying meat outdoors in the sun or indoors in a warm, well-ventilated space, keep in mind that ventilation is actually more important than temperature. The people of Greenland traditionally built stone meat drying huts with open-air "windows" on windy bluffs. The meat hung in such huts was dried solely by air flow. That said, direct sun or the heat generated by a furnace or wood stove will speed up the rate at which meat dries greatly.

Meat dried outdoors or indoors is usually hung, either on strings or wooden poles. You will want to make your slices as long as pos-

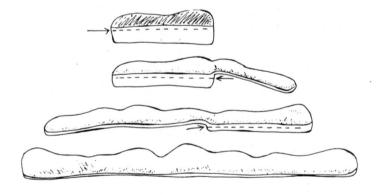

Butterfly cut for jerky making.

Strips of meat hanging to dry on a simple tripod.

sible—the longer the strips, the less strips you'll have to hang, tend, remove and make space for. By learning how to make slices as large as possible, one can easily make what would have been a dozen small strips into one continuous long strip.

Hang slices on strings, poles or racks in direct sun outdoors or, alternatively, indoors with a heat source. When drying meat outdoors, flies will inevitably come land on it; they won't eat your meat, but will lay eggs on it. In full sun, however, your meat should begin to form a *cuticle*—a dry outer rind that is inhospitable to maggots— quickly enough that they won't be an issue. If that isn't good enough for you, you can drape mosquito netting over your drying frame to keep flies and wasps out.

Once your meat has begun to visibly dry out, go to all the individual strips and open them up, ensuring that they aren't folded onto themselves on the inside, preventing full drying. In a warm, airy spot either indoors or outside, meat hung to dry in this way should be ready within roughly 24–72 hours, but no need to worry if it takes longer. Again, the test to see if it is done: when you bend it, it should break.

Marinades

One of the reasons people get so excited about jerky is because of the tasty marinades it can be infused with. I must admit, however, that I rarely ever marinate my meat before drying. Pretty much never, actually. I prefer the pure, unadulterated flavor of dried red meat, and find its flavor alone is more than adequate to keep me stimulated and satisfied. I do appreciate tasting some marinated jerky every once in a while though, and would be remiss if I didn't include a simple, delicious marinade here. This recipe is a slightly tweaked version of one that comes from author and nutrition expert Mark Sisson.

Ingredients

For about two pounds meat:
- ¼ cup soy sauce or tamari
- 2 tablespoons Worcestershire sauce
- 3 crushed garlic cloves
- 2 teaspoons onion powder
- 2 teaspoons hot chili powder
- ½–1 teaspoon each of salt and black pepper

Combine ingredients and marinate your sliced meat with them overnight in a plastic bag.

Parasites and dried meat

Depending on how you dry it, your jerky might technically be raw, which means you might feel a little worried about what parasites it could be carrying. If you are concerned, the best ways of dealing with this risk are either freezing your meat for fourteen days (according to the USDA, this eliminates any viable parasite risk from meat) or salting/marinating it. Any marinade with a good sodium or vinegar content will destroy parasites. To be doubly sure, Oregon State University recommends briefly dropping slices of meat into a boiling marinade before drying, just long enough for it to turn color and cook, but not so long that it becomes tough. This takes the place of an overnight marinade.

The meat from any omnivorous animal (pig, bear, raccoon, etc.) should definitely undergo these protective measures, as it can contain certain parasites that are quite dangerous to humans.

Smoking

Smoking meat is done less to preserve it and more to add a unique flavor. Foods like smoked ham, cold smoked salmon (lox) and other smoked meats that still have a high moisture content undergo a process called *cold smoking*. The large amounts of salt applied to these cuts of meat do more to preserve them than the smoke does, although the smoke also helps extend their shelf life. In the cold smoking process, a cool, smoky fire is maintained and smoke from it is funneled into a separate compartment where the meat is hung. This ensures that the heating effects of the fire do not directly reach the smoking meat; it remains cold in the smoker, and the resulting product is still somewhat moist. Smoked jerky and dry smoked salmon, on the other hand, undergo a process called *hot smoking*, which requires a low, smouldering fire maintained in the same area as the meat (a smoke house). Smoke houses are still common features in many native communities where wild fish and meat are a major part of people's diets. Hot smoking more actively preserves food, by both slowly drying it (the fire is never allowed to actually get *hot*, or it would cook the meat; instead it is kept at a low, smoky smoulder and has a gradual dehydrating effect) and by adding creosote, a powerful preservative. Creosote is also a powerful carcinogen, and as such, smoked meat should be eaten sparingly.

Hot smoking

Many people swear by their electric smokehouses, and I understand why. There is a convenient hot plate in them that one simply puts pans of dry wood chips on every once in a while; there is no risk of flare-ups that might burn all of the meat or the smokehouse down in a more traditional set-up (I've done this) and so no need to tirelessly monitor the smoker. If you don't want to buy one of these electric smokers, one can be easily improvised using an old, empty refrigerator and a hot plate. If the refrigerator has steel grated shelving, this will even serve as ideal, pre-made racks to hang strips of meat on. When using the electric smokehouse, you don't need to continually add fresh wood chips to the pan and keep it smoking. In fact, one of the great things about this system is that you can carefully decide just how much or little smoke to add to your food; the heat of the electric hot plate will continue dehydrating and preserving your meat without any fuel smoking it. One can make very nice, lightly smoked jerky this way.

A real smokehouse is easy to build or improvise if you don't have access to one. All you need is a fire pit, walls that will contain the smoke and protect your fire from gusts of wind, racks or strings to hang meat from well above the fire pit and a roof. You will want to leave a vent at the top of your structure for smoke to escape through.

I have made smokehouses using poles and tarps, plywood, metal roofing, slabs of cedar bark; they need not be fancy, but then again, if one is making a permanent smokehouse, it should be well built.

Your meat should hang on strings or racks at least five feet above the fire pit, and preferably higher. Begin a low fire in the smokehouse using some dry hardwood so that you get a good bed of coals. You can alternatively build a fire outside the smokehouse and move the coals into it with a shovel, to prevent any of your hanging meat from being cooked. Once you have a coal bed you have established a good solid *heart* to your fire and can begin adding fresh, green wood (again, use a hard wood here—maple, alder, apple, cherry are some of the best; resinous softwoods like cedar, spruce and pine will make your meat taste strongly of pitch) to the point that your fire is no longer producing any flame at all, just smouldering and emitting plenty of smoke. Now you're smoking. From this point on, you want the fire to maintain its coal bed and continue smouldering along, preferably with very few flames. Some people will take a metal trash can lid or piece of metal roofing and put it on top of the smouldering fire at this point, to ensure that if there is a flare-up, none of the flames will jump into the air above and touch the meat. Maintain the smokehouse like this until the meat is dry, feeding the fire, fanning the coals if they are getting weak and smothering them if they grow too lively.

Canning

Pressure canning is another great way of preserving meat, particularly those bits and scraps that are covered in tough connective tissue. These extra-chewy scraps become extremely tender through the process of pressure canning, resulting in wonderful, conveniently pre-cooked jars of meat that can be cracked open and added to stir fries, soups and other dishes. To pressure can chewy chunks of meat, chop up the chunks and fill sterile jars to within 1–1½ inches of the rim. Pack the meat down with a wooden spoon when doing this, to push out the oxygen. Clean off the rim, screw boiled lids on and process for 90 minutes at 10 psi (up to 2000 ft elevation; 15 psi from 2000–4000 ft). If you have a pressure canner, it should come with a small pamphlet describing its safe use and times/pressure for various items at various elevations. If not, look this information up. There isn't space to tackle the subject of pressure canning fully here, but you do need to familiarize yourself with it if you are going to do it safely. It is one of the only methods of preservation that can actually be deadly if you don't do it right.

Canning is also a great way of preserving bone broth. Unlike bits of meat, however, you'll have to prepare your broth and then put it into jars and can. The addition of a jar of broth can instantaneously transform a sauce, soup or other dish from something good into something *amazing*.

Ribs from larger creatures (deer-sized and up) can also be cut into chunks and pressure canned; letting them cook for a bit longer than the prescribed 90 minutes will result in the rib bones becoming "chalky" and edible (an excellent source of calcium). Likewise squirrels, rabbits and other wee animals can be canned whole with some chopped garlic, onion, salt and spices.

Burying

The methods of preservation listed above are all fairly well known and widely used around the world. There are, however, some other methods that have fallen almost entirely into obscurity. In times long past, for instance, hunter-gatherers in certain areas preserved whole mammoth legs by submerging them in peat bogs. The acidity of the water apparently helped induce a process of fermentation that resulted in the meat becoming pickled, quite literally. In other areas ashes or barrels of salt were employed. Another method that is very simple and practical, and which I have some experience with, is burying.

Meat buried one and a half to two feet deep in a patch of well-drained earth will be protected from flies, heat and drying, slowly ageing for weeks to months. I have tried this with whole rabbits that I buried for two weeks before making stew out of them; in each case the rabbit was tender and had a wonderful flavor.

To bury meat for storage, dig a hole to the depth specified above, in a spot that is well drained. Line this pit with a good, thick layer of leaves. Place your meat on these leaves and cover it with a very

A rabbit being buried for preservation.

thick layer of leaves. This will ensure no soil gets on the meat. Once the meat is sufficiently covered with foliage, fill the hole back in with soil. If there is a threat of dogs, bears or others digging up your treasure, place boards, rocks or other safeguards on top of it. The meat will now slowly age. Under most circumstances it can be stored for a month or two in this way. Throwing a few peeled cloves of garlic in with your buried meat can infuse it with a pleasant flavor over that time.

Afterword

I DON'T KNOW that I had ever before felt gratitude so deeply as the first time I killed a deer. I will never forget the moment I walked up to that motionless young buck lying on the forest floor, whose life I had just taken. His tongue was drooping out of his mouth, his dark eyes wide open, his face completely calm. As I looked at his face, I remember my eyes watering up and my entire body being flooded with an enormous *thank you*. I didn't know any ceremony to commemorate the moment, or have any tradition to reenact that might express my gratitude. But really, the feeling was enough.

For every meal I ate that he was a part of, every piece of dried meat that I snacked on while talking with a friend, I was filled with that gratitude, with a profound sense of thankfulness and awe at the beauty I was so fortunate to be eating. Thanks to that deer, I had meat to eat. And thanks to that deer, I had food that was sacred. It came from the magic of the land.

To eat something that is sacred is very interesting, since often in our culture something "sacred" is thought to be something that is untouched, untouchable; something that must exist outside of everyday earthly existence. Of course, since so many of us think this way, we have constructed a world, or a way of being in the world, that reflects this belief.

Most food hunters, regardless of their beliefs or ideals, have a strong sense that the food they harvest is sacred. The whole act is sacred. It also happens to be one of the most primal, earthly acts of subsistence that people still feel called to experience. A sanctity that is intertwined with daily living.

A question I've thought a lot about over the years is, How can one give thanks, or give back? Every time I have killed a creature, I have taken something extremely beautiful out of this world. I am acutely aware of this, and the gravity of it, because it was my doing.

I have never come up with a clear answer to this question. However, trying to honor the animal's body by using it all, and trying to live in a good way, using the energy I have gained from my food with integrity and honesty: all of these things seem to be very important parts of the answer.

Perhaps part of hunting, part of the journey of being alive and killing for our food, is revisiting this question of giving thanks again and again. Doing our best to figure it out and honor the amazing process of death, nourishment and rebirth that makes us alive.

APPENDIX A:
Resources

Natural hide tanning
Books
Deerskins to Buckskins by Matt Richards
This book is the definitive guide to making your own, naturally tanned buckskin leather. It is extremely user-friendly, with high-quality information that will allow the beginning tanner to produce the softest buckskin imaginable.

Leather: Tanning and Preparation by Traditional Methods by Lotta Rahme
This book is one of the best available books on the process of making full bodied, natural, bark-tanned leather. That's not saying much, though; there aren't really many books on this subject. Not very clear or user-friendly, it is still very interesting and one can figure out how to make bark-tanned leather by using it.

People
Smokin' Hides Traditional Tanning
This is my brother Lonnie's company, operated out of his backyard and workshop in Port Alberni, BC. He produces high-quality, traditionally bark-tanned leather, rawhide and fine, handmade natural leather crafts. He also teaches the bark-tan method of leather making. He's a wonderful guy, a great teacher, a knowledgeable outdoorsman and a skilled craftsman. Visit smokinhides.wordpress.com to find out more or send him an email (lonniemorse@yahoo.ca).

Preparing wild meat
Venison Cookbook by A. D. Livingston
This book stands out for its thorough, no-nonsense information on

using the entire creature. It is full of great ideas and recipes for wild venison. A great resource.

Tracking and sign

Tracking and the Art of Seeing: How to Read Animal Tracks and Sign by Paul Rezendes

Of the many guides to animal track and sign, Paul Rezendes' is one of the best I have come across. Rezendes is both a master tracker and a professional wildlife photographer, and the images, writing and quality of information in his book are all fantastic.

The Science and Art of Tracking by Tom Brown, Jr.

I've never actually been able to push myself into doing all the exercises in this book, or really dive into the material in a practical way, but it does stand out as one of the most ambitious and fascinating guides to tracking available.

Hunting, general

Caribou Hunter: A Song of a Vanished Life by Serge Bouchard

This book is a collection of stories told by Innu elder and hunter Mathieu Mestokosho to anthropologist Serge Bouchard. The stories detail a way of living on the land as nomadic hunters and trappers at a time when that way of life was changing rapidly. They are filled with honesty and beauty.

Eating Aliens by Jackson Landers

Jackson Landers is a naturalist, writer and hunting educator who details some of his experiences hunting various invasive species in this book. He is also the author of *The Beginner's Guide to Hunting Deer for Food*, another excellent resource for beginning hunters.

Bow Making

Books

The Traditional Bowyer's Bible (Volumes 1–4)

These books are filled with the clearest, most precise information on traditional bowmaking anywhere. If you are at all interested in making your own bow I strongly recommend getting either volume one or two of this series. You won't be disappointed.

People

Ravenbeak Natureworks

Based out of Powell River, BC, Jamie Macdonald and Jenna Fickes sell world-class, handcrafted yew wood bows as well as offering workshops where students craft their own yew wood bow from start to finish. Visit them online to find out more (www.ravenbeak.com).

APPENDIX B:
Regulations and Licensing

Hunting regulations vary widely from region to region, but wherever you live you will be required by law to obtain an appropriate licence and/or tags before doing most all hunting. A required hunter-education course is part of the licensing process, which especially for the beginner can provide some valuable practical insights and also information on the regional rules and regulations. The money you pay for your hunting license (and tags for individual animals) usually goes in part to fund conservation work and research that ensures the future health of wild animal populations.

Acknowledgments

I would like to thank everyone at New Society Publishers for your support in this project, in particular Ingrid Witvoet. A very brief conversation between us sparked what would later become this book. Many thanks to Scott Steedman for refining the book with your sharp editing skills.

I am also very grateful for the many friends, acquaintances, strangers and others who have taught, shared and otherwise contributed to my journey of learning how to harvest animals and honor their bodies by making the fullest use of them. There are countless teachers and peers who I have been blessed to learn from. Thank you.

My sincere gratitude to my family and to a handful of amazing, precious friends with whom I have had the opportunity to share some of the wonder and beauty of life as well as the ideas churning in me while writing this.

Most of all, I thank any creature whose life I have taken and whose body has fed me in many ways. The sense of gratitude I feel in this is beyond words.

Index

Page numbers in *italics* indicate diagrams.

About the Author

MILES OLSON has spent the better part of a decade living off the grid and intimately on the land, as a squatter on the forested edge of a sprawling town on Vancouver island. Subsisting by foraging, hunting, scavenging, gardening and scrounging as part of a small community of feral homesteaders, he has amassed a toolkit of various earth based living skills, as well as a unique perspective on the relationship between humanity and wild nature.

If you have enjoyed *The Compassionate Hunter's Guidebook*,
you might also enjoy other

BOOKS TO BUILD A NEW SOCIETY

Our books provide positive solutions for people who want to
make a difference. We specialize in:

**Sustainable Living • Green Building • Peak Oil
Renewable Energy • Environment & Economy
Natural Building & Appropriate Technology
Progressive Leadership • Resistance and Community
Educational & Parenting Resources**

New Society Publishers

ENVIRONMENTAL BENEFITS STATEMENT

New Society Publishers has chosen to produce this book on recycled paper made
with **100% post consumer waste**, processed chlorine free, and old growth free.

For every 5,000 books printed, New Society saves the following resources:[1]

20	Trees
1,833	Pounds of Solid Waste
2,016	Gallons of Water
2,630	Kilowatt Hours of Electricity
3,332	Pounds of Greenhouse Gases
14	Pounds of HAPs, VOCs, and AOX Combined
5	Cubic Yards of Landfill Space

[1]Environmental benefits are calculated based on research done by the Environmental Defense Fund
and other members of the Paper Task Force who study the environmental impacts of the paper
industry.

For a full list of NSP's titles, please call 1-800-567-6772 *or check out our website* at:

www.newsociety.com

new society
PUBLISHERS